Birthday and Special Occasions

Strawberry Shortcake

See photo on page 3

DECORATING NEEDS

- 8-inch layer cake
- 10-inch foil-covered board
- 3 recipes Buttercream Icing (3 cups Royal Red, 2 cups Leaf Green, ½ cup Yellow, ½ cup Brown, ¼ cup Pink, remaining White)
- Tips 1, 2, 4, 6, 10, 16, 32, 101, 233, 350
- Flower Nail #2
- Waxed paper
- 1 muffin or cupcake

REVIEW TECHNIQUES

- Shell border
- Leaves and stems
- Flower blossoms (violets)
- Stars

INSTRUCTIONS
---

1. At least 1 day in advance, make Strawberry Shortcake. Make 40 tip 101 violets with tip 1 yellow and green dot centers. (Can be made with Buttercream or Royal Icing.)

2. Ice cake on foil-covered board.

3. Make green grass with tip 233, holding the tip perpendicular to the cake and applying heavy pressure to attach, decreasing pressure as tip is pulled away from cake.

4. Pipe a tip 32 bottom shell border and a tip 16 top shell border.

5. Pipe a tip 2 flowing stem line around side of cake. Attach tip 350 leaves and violets. Pipe on tip 6 strawberries. When strawberries have formed a crust, trim berries with black dots. Decorate base of cake with berries, leaves, and violets.

6. Stand the muffin or cupcake on top of cake. Cover with tip 32 stars. Outline door with tip 4. Fill in door with tip 16 stars. Pipe a tip 16 star window on front of door and make two windows. Outline windows with tip 4.

7. Fill parchment bag with leaf green icing. Cut a large "V" tip. Pipe leaves on top of strawberry house. Pipe a large tip 10 stem.

8. Pipe tip 233 grass where Strawberry Shortcake figure is to stand. Stand figure in wet icing.

CREATIVE COOKBOOK SERIES

SPECIAL OCCASION CAKE DECORATING

VI BRAND WHITTINGTON

ideals

Ideals Publishing Corp.
Milwaukee, Wisconsin

Contents

Supplies are available wherever cake decorating supplies are sold or write to:

The Country Store
2255 CR 27
Waterloo, Indiana 46793

For more cake decorating ideas and instructions see "Easy Cake Decorating" by Mildred Brand, published by Ideals Publishing Corp.

Ted E. Bear from *The Bear Who Slept through Christmas*, copyright 1980, Dimenmark Inc.

Patti Bear from *The Easter Bear*, copyright 1981, Dimenmark Inc.

Thingumajig from *The Thingumajig Book of Manners*, copyright 1981, Dick and Irene Keller.

ISBN 0-8249-3028-2
Copyright © MCMLXXXIV by Ideals Publishing Corp.
All rights reserved.
Printed and bound in the United States of America.

Published by Ideals Publishing Corporation
11315 Watertown Plank Road
Milwaukee, Wisconsin 53226
Published simultaneously in Canada

Cover Cakes:
Ziggy, 9
New Addition to the Family, 24
Easter Wishes, 50
Santa and His Elves, 54

Strawberry Shortcake, 4
Circus Clowns, 5

HOW TO FIGURE PIPE STRAWBERRY SHORTCAKE

DECORATING NEEDS

1 recipe Royal Icing (¼ cup each:
   Coppertone, Royal Red, Orange, Black, Pink,
   Avocado, Lemon Yellow)
Tips 1, 2, 5, 6, 101s
Waxed paper
Fine artist brush

Step 1 *Neck* Pipe neck with tip 2 in a bag of flesh-colored icing.

Step 2 *Head* Make the face by holding the bag straight up about ⅛ inch above the surface and forming a ball. While maintaining steady pressure, move tip to the right, then left to form cheeks and then down for the chin.

Step 3 *Body* Make the body with tip 6 in red icing. Begin at the shoulders and increase pressure, moving back and forth and increasing pressure to form the skirt.

Step 4 *Arms* Make arms with tip 6, beginning at the shoulder and increasing pressure slightly as arms form.

Step 5 *Hands, Hair, Legs* Make the hands with tip 1 forming balls at ends of arms. Insert tip into ball and pull out with slight pressure to form thumbs and fingers. Make hair with tip 2 and orange icing, using a circular motion to form curls.

Step 6 *Hat, Apron, Features* Make tip 6 hat in pink icing. Make the hatband with tip 6 in red icing, and the bill with tip 6 in pink icing. Pipe tip 1 strawberries. To form strawberries, apply heavy pressure, and move tip back and forth slightly, decreasing pressure. Pipe tip 1 stems with green icing. Use tip 101s to pipe the apron. Pipe tip 1 hearts on the apron with red icing. Use a fine artist brush to add facial details and to paint stripes on stockings and shoes.

Circus Clowns

See photo on page 3

DECORATING NEEDS

8-inch layer cake
10-inch foil-covered board
3 recipes Buttercream Icing (2 cups Yellow, 2 cups Red, remaining White)
Food color: Royal Blue, Royal Red, Lemon Yellow
White candy coating (½ pound)
Colored candy coating; 15 wafers *each*: blue, red, pink, green, orange, yellow, black
Clear plastic balloon mold or plastic balloon decoration
4 small plastic clown picks
2 lollipop sticks
Decorating Tips 2, 4, 6, 16, 32, 102

REVIEW TECHNIQUES

Star border
Wiggle border
Strings
Dots
Chocolate painting and molding

INSTRUCTIONS

1. Make 6 chocolate molded balloon clusters, using lollipop sticks for 2 of the clusters.
2. Ice cake on foil-covered board.
3. Pipe a bottom tip 32 star border.
4. Pipe a top tip 16 wiggle border and tip 16 side string border.
5. Use tip 4 and red icing to make the following: center dots on bottom border stars and small arches on inside top of cake.
6. Make clowns as directed below.
7. Insert a plastic pick in each clown.

HOW TO FIGURE PIPE CLOWNS

DECORATING NEEDS

Tips 2, 4, 32, 102
Paste food color: Red, Yellow, Blue
Artist brushes

Clowns can be made ahead on waxed paper using Royal Icing. To make directly on the cake, use Buttercream or Boiled Icing. A lying down clown or one standing against the cake can be made with either icing. A sit-down clown should be made with Royal or Boiled Icing. Buttercream Icing can be used, but since it is soft, place a block or some other small toy behind the clown to prevent it from falling.

Step 1   Use a parchment bag fitted with tip 32. Using red, yellow, and blue paste food color, paint a wide lengthwise line one-third of the way around the inside of the bag. Fill with white icing.

Step 2   *Sit-down clown*   Using prepared bag, hold perpendicular to surface and apply heavy pressure to make "seat" of clown. Move tip up and down in short, quick movements, decreasing pressure as desired height is reached.

Step 2A   *Lying down or standing clown*   Hold tip at a 45° angle and apply light pressure to make the neck, gradually increasing pressure as the tip is moved down in short, quick movements toward the "seat."

Step 3   *Arms and Legs*   Insert tip 32 into shoulder. Apply pressure, moving the tip up and down in short, quick movements and keeping steady pressure until desired length is reached. Form legs as for arms.

Step 4   *Hands*   Use tip 2 and blue icing to make a small ball at the end of each arm. Insert the tip inside the ball and draw out thumb and fingers.

Step 5   *Shoes*   Use tip 4 and black icing to form a ball at the heel, applying moderate pressure and moving tip until desired length is reached, increasing pressure to form the rounded top of the shoe.

Step 6   *Ruffles*   Use tip 102 and white icing. Insert the large end of the tip lightly into the top of the body. Move tip in a zigzag motion, always touching the top of the body with the large end of the tip. Work completely around the top of the body. Repeat for ruffles around arms and legs.

Ziggy

Ziggy Character Design
© 1984 Universal Press Syndicate
Copied with the permission of Universal Press Syndicate
See photo on page 6

DECORATING NEEDS

13 x 9-inch sheet cake
14 x 10-inch foil-covered board
2 recipes Buttercream Icing (2½ cups Gold, remaining White)
24 Royal Icing Ziggys
Tips 2, 16, 32
Food color: Gold

REVIEW TECHNIQUES

Shell border
Strings
Bulb and drop border

─── INSTRUCTIONS ───

1. At least 1 day in advance, make 24 Ziggys.
2. Ice a cake on foil-covered board.
3. Pipe a tip 32 bottom shell border.
4. Use a long spatula to lightly mark cake top into 24 squares.
5. Pipe a tip 16 shell border around each square.
6. Pipe a tip 2 string border around bottom.
7. Pipe a tip 2 bulb and drop border around top of cake.
8. Place Ziggy figures in centers of squares, securing each with a small amount of icing.

HOW TO FIGURE
PIPE ZIGGY

DECORATING NEEDS

½ recipe Royal Icing (1 cup Gold, 1 cup Coppertone)
Tips 2, 6
Fine artist brush
Black paste color

Step 1 *Body* Pipe neck with tip 6 in a bag of gold icing. Hold tip at a 45° angle and apply light pressure, moving the tip down and increasing pressure to form the body. Release pressure and pull tip away.

Step 2 *Arms* Still using tip 6, insert tip into shoulder at a 45° angle. Apply light pressure and move tip down to form arm, increasing pressure until desired length is reached. Release pressure and pull tip away.

Step 3 *Head and Feet* With tip 6 in a bag of flesh-colored icing, hold tip above neck and centered between shoulders, about ⅛ inch from surface. Apply pressure and form head, holding bag steady. Release pressure and pull tip away. Make feet in the same way the head was made.

Step 4 *Features* With tip 2 in flesh-colored icing, make 4 dots at the end of each arm for fingers. Near the top of the head, make a dot for the nose. Use black paste color and an artist brush to paint eyes and mouth.

Party Petit Fours

DECORATING NEEDS

1 recipe Molded Petit Fours

For Pastel Petit Fours

1 recipe molded petit fours coated with your choice of colored candy coating
Royal Icing (Green, White, Pink, Blue, Yellow)
Tips 1, 2, 101s, 349
Flower nail #2
Waxed paper squares

For Christmas Petit Fours

1 recipe Molded Petit Fours coated with red and green candy coating
Royal Icing (your choice of Christmas colors)
Tips 1, 349

REVIEW TECHNIQUES

Roses
Leaves and stems
Dots
How to Figure Pipe Ducks (page 25)

REVIEW TECHNIQUES

Stems and leaves
Poinsettias
Dots

INSTRUCTIONS

1. Prepare petit fours following directions on page 11.

2. Decorate as desired for pastel or Christmas petit fours.

Chocolate Molded Petit Fours

    1 recipe favorite pound cake
    1 pound colored candy coating
    2½ tablespoons paramont crystals
    Your choice filling, such as pudding, preserves
        or commercial filling

1. Bake pound cake in an 8-inch square pan following recipe directions. Cool in pan 10 minutes before turning out onto a wire rack to cool completely.

2. Melt candy coating with paramont crystals, stirring to dissolve.

3. Line petit four mold thinly with coating. Chill.

4. Cut cake into 1-inch squares. Trim brown crust from cake and slice crosswise into thirds.

5. Fill lined mold with cake and filling, beginning with filling and ending with cake. For ease in filling molds, fill a decorating bag fitted with tip 7 with filling and pipe into molds.

6. Seal with coating. Chill in freezer. Pop out of mold. Trim bottom edges with scissors, if necessary.

7. Decorate as desired following directions below.

Pastel Petit Fours

1. At least 1 day in advance, pipe tip 101s roses. (For last-minute work, dry roses in the oven for 20 minutes at 100° F.)

2. Attach roses to petit fours with dots of icing. Pipe tip 340 leaves and tip 2 stems.

3. For lilies of the valley, pipe tip 2 dots and add stems.

4. For swans, follow directions for piping duck, making the neck longer.

Christmas Petit Fours

1. To make candles, use tip 1 and desired colors.

2. To make wreaths, use tip 349 and trim with tip 1 berries and bows.

3. To make bells, use tip 1 to make a spiral. Trim with tip 1 dots for clappers.

4. To make trees, use tip 349 and trim as desired.

5. To make poinsettias, use tip 340 and trim with tip 1 centers.

6. To make Santa Claus, follow directions on page 52, using tips 1 size smaller.

Swirl Petit Fours

    1 recipe favorite cake
    ½ cup butter or margarine
    ½ cup vegetable shortening
    2 cups powdered sugar
    ⅓ cup unsweetened cocoa
    1 pound chocolate coating
    1½ tablespoons paramont crystals

Prepare cake recipe and bake in greased miniature muffin cups. Set aside to cool. In a large mixing bowl, cream butter and shortening until light and fluffy. Gradually add powdered sugar and cocoa, beating until well blended. Spoon mixture into a decorating bag fitted with a coupler only. Pipe mound of powdered cocoa mixture on top of each cake. Chill. Melt coating and paramont crystals, stirring to dissolve. Dip cakes in melted coating.

Almond Coconut Petit Fours

    1 package (8 ounces) almond paste
    1 cup butter, softened
    1 cup sugar
    5 eggs, divided
    ⅞ cup cake flour, sifted
    Raspberry jam
    Dessicated coconut
    Whole or slivered almonds

Line a 12 x 18-inch baking pan with parchment paper and grease lightly; set aside. Preheat oven to 350° F. In a large mixing bowl, combine almond paste and 1 egg; blend well. Add butter and sugar; beat until smooth. Add remaining eggs, 1 at a time, beating well after each addition. Blend in cake flour. Spread mixture in prepared pan. Bake on top rack of oven until light brown and a wooden pick inserted in the center comes out clean. Remove from oven. Place a sheet of waxed paper over top of cake. Turn out of pan onto waxed paper. Peel off parchment paper. Let stand 15 minutes. Turn cake over and peel off waxed paper. Cut cake crosswise in half. Spread one half with raspberry jam. Place remaining cake half on top of jam. Chill for 1 hour. Cut into small squares. Brush sides and tops with raspberry jam. Roll in dessicated coconut. Garnish each with a whole or slivered almond.

Sixteenth Birthday

See photo on page 6

DECORATING NEEDS

1 sheet rice paper (8 x 11 inch)
Piping gel
Artist brushes: 1½ inch and size 0
9 x 13-inch sheet cake
10 x 14-inch foil-covered board
2 recipes Buttercream Icing (1 recipe Lemon Yellow,
   1 recipe Royal Red)
Food color: Lemon Yellow, Royal Red, Royal Blue,
   Leaf Green
Tips 1, 16, 32

REVIEW TECHNIQUES

Shell border
Reverse scroll border
Piping gel pictures
Writing

INSTRUCTIONS

1. Trace pattern opposite on rice paper. Paint with piping gel.
2. Ice cake on foil-covered board.
3. Pipe tip 32 shell borders around bottom and top of cake.

4. Place rice paper with drawing on top of cake.
5. Pipe a tip 16 reverse scroll border around the rice paper.
6. Pipe tip 1 message on top of cake.

Sportsman's Cake

See photo on page 14

DECORATING NEEDS

8-inch layer cake
10-inch foil-covered board
½ recipe Royal Icing (divided and colored Gold, Light
   Brown, Brown, Leaf Green, Black, and White)
2 recipes Buttercream Icing (3 cups Brown, 1 cup White)
1 cup piping gel: Blue
Food color: Brown, Leaf Green, Gold, Black, Royal Blue
Tips 2, 16, 32, 352
Fine artist brush

REVIEW TECHNIQUES

Run sugar
Shell border
Leaves and stems
Writing

INSTRUCTIONS

1. At least 1 day in advance, make run sugar duck, outlining with tip 2 black royal icing and filling in with thinned colors as listed.
2. Ice cake on foil-covered board with white buttercream icing.
3. Pipe a bottom tip 32 shell border.
4. Thin royal blue food color with a little water. Use a brush to blend thinned food color into icing to make the sky.

5. Spread piping gel over bottom half of cake for water.
6. Place run sugar duck on the water.
7. Pipe tip 2 stems and cattails with brown icing. Pipe tip 352 leaves.
8. Make a double tip 16 top shell border.
9. Pipe tip 2 message on top of cake.

Special Hobby Cake

See photo on page 7

DECORATING NEEDS

1 sheet rice paper
Piping gel
Artist brushes
12-inch layer cake
14-inch foil-covered board
½ recipe Royal Icing (½ cup Lemon Yellow, remainder Violet)
Tips 1, 16, 32, 101, 350
Flower Nail #2
Waxed paper
Food color: Brown, Red, Lemon Yellow, Violet, Leaf Green
3 recipes Buttercream Icing (1 cup Leaf Green, remaining White)

REVIEW TECHNIQUES

Piping gel pictures
Flower blossoms (violets)
Shell border
Scroll border
Writing

INSTRUCTIONS
---

1. At least 1 day in advance, trace horse pattern on page 15 onto rice paper. (Or, use any picture of a favorite pet or hobby.) Paint with piping gel. After piping gel has dried, trim picture.

2. At least 4 hours in advance, make 72 tip 101 violets with Royal Icing and tip 1 yellow centers. (For last-minute work, dry flowers in oven for 20 minutes at 100° F.)

3. Ice cake on foil-covered board.

4. Pipe a tip 16 top shell border and a tip 32 bottom shell border.

5. Place rice paper with drawing on top of cake.

6. Pipe tip 1 stems and tip 350 leaves.

7. Attach violets at bases of leaves and around bottom border.

8. Pipe tip 1 message on top of cake.

Woodland Scene, 17
Sportsman's Cake, 12

Pattern for Woodland Scene

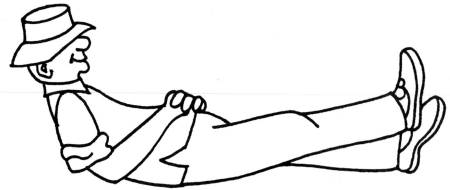

Pattern for Just Swingin'

Woodland Scene

See photo on page 14

DECORATING NEEDS

10-inch layer cake
12-inch foil-covered board
½ recipe Royal Icing (divided into thirds — ⅓ cup Brown, ⅓ cup Black, ⅓ cup White)
2 recipes Buttercream Icing (½ cup Mulberry, 1 cup Leaf Green, ½ cup Mint Green, remainder divided into Royal Blue and Brown)
Piping gel — Blue

Food color: Brown, Black, Mulberry, Leaf Green, Royal Blue, Mint Green
Tips 2, 6, 32, 233, 352
Fine artist brushes

REVIEW TECHNIQUES

Run sugar
Leaves and stems
Shell border

INSTRUCTIONS

---

1. At least 1 day in advance make run sugar deer with Royal Icing, outlining with tip 2 and black icing and filling in with thinned brown and white.
2. Ice cake on foil-covered board with light blue icing on the top and brown on the sides.
3. Pipe tip 6 mulberry mountains. Smooth with a knife. Pipe tip 6 trees in blue icing.

4. Fill a parchment bag with blue piping gel. Pipe gel on top of cake to make a lake.
5. Pipe tip 233 grass around the lake.
6. Place run sugar deer on top of cake.
7. Pipe tip 6 tree trunk and branches. Pipe tip 352 leaves.
8. Pipe a tip 32 bottom and top shell border.

Just Swingin'

See photo on page 20

DECORATING NEEDS

8-inch layer cake
10-inch foil-covered board
½ recipe Royal Icing (divided equally and colored Grey, Lemon Yellow, Purple, Coppertone, Brown, Black)
2 recipes Buttercream Icing (2 cups Light Royal Blue, remainder White, Brown, Leaf Green)
Tips 2, 6, 32, 233, 352
Food color: Royal Blue, Leaf Green, Brown, Lemon Yellow, Purple, Coppertone, Black

REVIEW TECHNIQUES

Run sugar
Leaves
Strings
Shell border

INSTRUCTIONS

---

1. At least 1 day in advance, make run sugar man with Royal Icing as listed.
2. Ice cake on foil-covered board with light royal blue icing.
3. Pipe tip 233 grass.
4. Pipe tip 6 tree trunks and branches.

5. Pipe tip 352 leaves on branches.
6. Place run sugar man between tree trunks. Pipe tip 2 strings between hammock and tree trunks and under run sugar man.
7. Pipe tip 32 top and bottom shell borders.

Cardinal Cake

See photo on page 19

DECORATING NEEDS

10-inch layer cake
12-inch foil-covered board
½ recipe Royal Icing (divided and colored Black, Gold, Royal Red, Green)
3 recipes Buttercream Icing (1 cup Brown, 1½ cups Royal Red, ½ cup Leaf Green, remaining Light Royal Blue)
Waxed paper
Food color: Royal Red, Leaf Green, Royal Blue, Gold, Black, Brown
Tips 1, 2, 4, 16

REVIEW TECHNIQUES

Run sugar
Shell border
Reverse scroll border
Stems
Writing

INSTRUCTIONS

---

1. At least 1 day in advance, make run sugar cardinal, outlining with tip 2 black royal icing and filling in with thinned gold and royal red icing. Do *not* thin the green icing. Store green icing in an airtight container for later use.

2. Ice cake on foil-covered board with light royal blue buttercream icing.

3. Pipe a tip 16 top and bottom shell border.

4. Pipe a tip 2 reverse scroll border on side of cake.

5. Pipe large tip 4 branches. Cover branches with tip 1 needles using reserved royal green icing. Hold tip perpendicular to branch and apply heavy pressure to attach, decreasing pressure as tip is pulled straight up to break off.

6. Place run sugar cardinal on branch.

7. Pipe tip 2 message on top of cake.

Daisies for Mother

See photo on page 22

DECORATING NEEDS

8-inch layer cake
10-inch foil-covered board
½ recipe Royal Icing (½ cup Yellow, remainder Pink)
2 recipes Buttercream Icing (1 cup Cherry Pink, 1 cup Mint Green, 1 cup Lemon Yellow, remainder White)
Flower Nail #7
Waxed paper
Tips 2, 4, 16, 32, 352
Food color: Cherry Pink, Mint Green, Lemon Yellow

REVIEW TECHNIQUES

Daisies
Reverse scroll border
Shell border
Strings
Writing
Leaves

— INSTRUCTIONS —

1. At least 1 day in advance make 12 tip 104 daisies with Royal Icing. Pipe tip 4 centers with yellow icing. (For last-minute work, dry flowers in oven for 20 minutes at 100° F.)
2. Ice cake on foil-covered board.
3. Pipe a 16 top reverse scroll border. Pipe tip 16 strings around the top edge. Pipe a tip 32 bottom shell border.

4. Pipe a tip 352 mound of icing in the center of the cake. Arrange daisies on wet icing. Pipe tip 352 leaves around daisies.
5. Pipe tip 2 message on top of cake.

Pansy Bouquet

See photo on page 22

DECORATING NEEDS

8-inch layer cake
10-inch foil-covered board
½ recipe Royal Icing (½ cup Lemon Yellow, remainder White)
Fine artist brush
2 recipes Buttercream Icing (2 cups Light Lemon Yellow, ½ cup Purple, remainder White)
Food color: Lemon Yellow, Purple, Leaf Green
Flower Nail #7
Tips 1, 32, 44, 104, 352

REVIEW TECHNIQUES

Pansies
Frame border
Shell border
Leaves and stems
Writing

1. At least 1 day in advance make 4 tip 104 yellow royal icing pansies and 3 white pansies. (For last-minute work, dry flowers in oven for 20 minutes at 100° F.) After pansies have dried, use an artist brush to paint centers and edges with purple food color.
2. Ice cake on a foil-covered board.
3. Pipe a tip 32 bottom shell border. Fill between shells with tip 44.

4. Pipe a tip 104 top frame border.
5. Pipe tip 1 stems on top of cake.
6. Arrange dried pansies on stems. Pipe tip 352 leaves around pansies.
7. Pipe tip 44 ribbon at base of pansies. Edge ribbon with tip 1.
8. Pipe tip 1 message on top of cake.

Roses for Mother

See photo on page 23

DECORATING NEEDS

12-inch layer cake
14-inch foil-covered board
⅓ recipe Royal Icing (Scarlet Red)
Flower Nail #7
Waxed paper
Food color: Scarlet Red, Leaf Green
2½ recipes Buttercream Icing (2 cups Leaf Green, remainder White)
Tips 2, 16, 32, 104, 352

REVIEW TECHNIQUES

Roses and rosebuds
Leaves and stems
Wiggle border
Shell border
Strings
Writing

1. At least 1 day in advance make 8 tip 104 roses with Royal or Buttercream Icing. Or, dry in oven for 20 minutes at 100° F. Make 1 tip 104 rosebud.
2. Ice cake on foil-covered board.
3. Pipe tip 2 stems on top of cake. Attach dried roses with dots of icing.
4. Pipe tip 352 leaves around rose arrangement.
5. Pipe tip 16 wiggle border on side of cake,

increasing and decreasing pressure to make fluffy-looking swags.
6. Pipe tip 16 top and a tip 32 bottom shell border.
7. Pipe tip 2 string border over and below the wiggle border.
8. Pipe tip 2 message on top of cake.

Congratulations Cakes

New Addition to the Family

See photo on page 26

DECORATING NEEDS

- 8-inch layer cake
- 10-inch foil-covered board
- 2 recipes Buttercream Icing (1 cup Leaf Green, 1 cup Brown, 1 cup Lemon Yellow, ½ cup Orange, remainder White)
- Fine artist brush: ½ inch and a fine brush
- 1 cup piping gel: Blue
- Paste food color: Lemon Yellow, Orange, Leaf Green, Brown, Royal Blue
- Tips 2, 4, 6, 16, 10 ls, 352

REVIEW TECHNIQUES

- Reverse scroll border
- Shell border
- Stems and leaves

───────────── **INSTRUCTIONS** ─────────────

1. Ice cake on foil-covered board.
2. Make sunset sky by dipping ½-inch brush into thinned royal blue paste color. Blend coloring into icing. Clean brush and dip into thinned yellow paste color. Blend yellow into blue icing.
3. Pipe tip 6 mountains. Smooth with a spatula.
4. Make the lake by spreading blue piping gel over icing.
5. Pipe tip 4 trunk and branches. Pipe tip 352 leaves on the tree.
6. Pipe tip 2 cattail stems, tip 352 leaves, and tip 6 cattail heads.
7. Pipe ducks directly on top of cake as shown opposite.
8. Pipe ducks on sides of cake. Pipe tip 2 water under ducks.
9. Pipe tip 32 bottom shell border and tip 16 top scroll border.
10. Pipe tip 2 message on top of cake.

HOW TO
FIGURE PIPE DUCKS

DECORATING NEEDS

Tips 6, 101s
Fine artist brush
Black food color

Step 1 *Head* Hold tip 6 perpendicular to surface. Apply moderate pressure to form head, moving downward to form neck.

Step 2 *Body* Hold tip at base of neck perpendicular to surface. Apply moderate pressure to form body, decreasing pressure to form a point at tip of tail.

Step 3 *Wing* Insert tip 6 into body. Apply pressure and pull out top to form a wing, decreasing pressure to form a wing tip.

Step 4 *Beak and Feet* Pipe beak with tip 101s, holding the wide end down and applying pressure while moving up slightly and then

releasing pressure to form tip. Repeat procedure for feet.

Step 5 Use artist brush to paint in black eyes.

It's a Girl!

See photo on page 26

DECORATING NEEDS

9 x 12-inch sheet cake
10 x 14-inch foil-covered board
2 recipes Buttercream Icing (1 recipe Light Royal Blue, 1 recipe Cherry Pink)
Royal Icing Heads
Food colors: Royal Blue, Cherry Pink, Coppertone, Brown, Lemon Yellow
Tips 4, 16

REVIEW TECHNIQUES

Star border
Scroll border
Bulb and drop border

─────── **INSTRUCTIONS** ───────

Note: Colors can be changed for a baby boy cake.

1. At least 1 day in advance, make 16 heads using Royal Icing following directions below.
2. Ice cake on foil-covered board.
3. Pipe a tip 16 shell border with blue icing near the bottom of the cake. Pipe a tip 16 pink shell border below blue shell border.

4. Use a long spatula to lightly mark top of cake into 16 pieces. Pipe a tip 16 reverse scroll border over markings. Pipe a bulb and drop border around the top edge with tip 4.
5. Pipe babies with Buttercream Icing following directions below.

25

HOW TO
FIGURE PIPE BABIES

DECORATING NEEDS

Tips 1, 6

Step 1 *Body* Form body with tip 6 by holding the bag at a 45° angle and applying light pressure while moving the tip down and increasing pressure to form the body. Release pressure and pull tip away.

Step 2 *Legs* Insert tip 6 into one side of lower body at a 45° angle. Apply pressure and move tip away from body to form leg. Increase pressure at base of leg to form a foot. Release pressure and pull tip away.

Step 3 *Arms* Insert tip 6 into one side of shoulder at a 45° angle. Apply pressure and move tip away from shoulder to form arm.

Step 4 *Hood and Features* Holding tip 6 perpendicular to and ⅛ inch above the surface, apply pressure without moving tip until desired size hood is obtained. Release pressure and pull tip away. Press a dried Royal Icing head into icing. Use tip 1 to pipe bows on the feet, ruffles around the hood, and a bow at the neck.

HOW TO MAKE
ROYAL ICING HEADS

Royal Icing heads can be used with any figure piped character. Make a whole tray at a time and let dry at least 15 hours. Store heads in a tightly covered container until needed. One recipe of Royal Icing will yield about 1000 heads.

DECORATING NEEDS

Royal Icing (Coppertone or Bronze for flesh color)
Waxed paper
Tip 2
Artist brushes 0, 8
Paste food color: Black, Pink, Coppertone, or Bronze, your choice hair color

Step 1 Thin icing by adding a small amount of water at a time and blending until icing smooths itself in 8 to 10 seconds when dropped onto waxed paper.

Step 2 Secure a large sheet of waxed paper to a tray with dots of icing. Pipe tip 2 dots onto tray allowing enough room between each for spreading. Let stand 10 minutes or until icing forms a crust.

Step 3 Pipe small dots onto centers to form noses. Let stand until icing forms a crust. (If making heads other than babies, include Step 3A.)

Step 3A Moisten the #8 artist brush with your choice of paste food color for hair. Wipe excess paste from brush with paper towel. Working with the heads upside down and beginning at the base of the head (neck), brush a single stroke to form hair and bangs.

Step 4 Thin a little black paste color with water until it is thin enough to make very fine lines using the #0 brush. Paint eyes on faces.

Step 5 Thin pink paste color as in Step 4. Paint mouths on faces.

Rainbow of Happiness

See photo on page 30

DECORATING NEEDS

9 x 13-inch sheet cake
10 x 14-inch foil-covered board
2 recipes Royal Icing (½ cup White, ½ cup Black,
   ½ cup Brown, ½ cup school color, ⅛ cup Coppertone,
   remainder divided into Yellow, Orange, Red,
   Blue, Purple)
Food color: Black, Brown, school colors, Coppertone,
   Yellow, Orange, Red, Blue, Purple
Tips 2, 16

REVIEW TECHNIQUES

Run sugar
Reverse scroll border
Shell border
Writing

INSTRUCTIONS

1. At least 1 day in advance, make the run sugar raccoon with Royal Icing, reserving remaining icing in a tightly covered container for later use. Outline raccoon with tip 2 and black icing. Fill in with thinned icing as shown.
2. Ice cake on a foil-covered board with Buttercream Icing.
3. Make 5 parchment bags with ½-inch

openings. Fill each bag with one of the rainbow colors. Beginning at the left side of the cake, form an arch of color for the rainbow. Repeat for remaining colors.
4. Place run sugar raccoon on top of cake.
5. Pipe a tip 32 bottom shell border and a tip 16 top scroll border.
6. Pipe tip 2 message on top of cake.

Graduation Hat

See photo on page 30

DECORATING NEEDS

6- or 8-inch layer cake
10- or 12-inch foil-covered board
2 recipes Buttercream Icing (color in your school's colors)
10- or 12-inch cardboard square
Tips 2, 3, 10, 16
Plastic graduate
Paper diploma with ribbon

REVIEW TECHNIQUES

Strings
Writing
Dots
Shell border

INSTRUCTIONS

1. Ice cake on foil-covered board.
2. Place cardboard over top of cake. Ice with thinned icing. Pipe a tip 16 shell border around edge of cardboard.
3. Pipe tip 3 strings to form a tassel. Pipe a tip 10 dot at top of tassel.

4. Attach diploma to top of cardboard with a dot of icing. Stand graduate on cardboard.
5. Pipe tip 2 message on cardboard.

Graduation March

See photo on page 30

DECORATING NEEDS

9 x 12-inch cake
12 x 18-inch cake
14 x 19-inch foil-covered board
6 recipes Buttercream Icing (color in your school's colors)
1 recipe Royal Icing (2 cups in desired color for roses, remainder Green)
12 4½-inch lollipop sticks
Green floral tape
12 1½-inch styrofoam balls
Tips 2, 16, 32, 101s, 350
Flower nail #2

Waxed paper
Food colors: as desired
Ribbon
Plastic graduate

REVIEW TECHNIQUES

Roses
Leaves
Shell border
Strings
Reverse scroll border
Writing

INSTRUCTIONS

1. At least 4 hours in advance, make 36 tip 101s miniature roses using Royal Icing.
2. Wrap lollipop sticks with floral tape. Push 1 stick into a styrofoam ball. Press stick with ball into a large block of styrofoam to steady while decorating.
3. Cover balls with tip 350 leaves using Royal Icing. Arrange roses on wet icing.
4. Ice the 12 x 18-inch cake on the foil-covered board. Place the 9 x 13-inch cake on top with one edge aligned with back edge as shown in photo.

5. Ice the top cake. Place a piece of ribbon down the center of the cakes to create an "aisle." Attach with dots of icing.
6. Pipe tip 32 vertical elongated shells around base of each cake. Pipe tip 2 strings over shells.
7. Pipe tip 16 reverse scroll border around the top of each cake.
8. Press trees into cake as shown in photo. Stand graduate on top of cake.
9. Pipe tip 2 message on top of cake.

Diploma Cake

DECORATING NEEDS

9 x 13-inch sheet cake
10 x 14-inch foil-covered board
½ recipe Royal Icing or Flower Decorator Icing (school colors)
2 recipes Buttercream Icing (2 cups White, divided into school colors and Leaf Green)
Parchment diploma
Plastic graduation hat
Flower Nail #7

Tips 2, 16, 32, 104, 350
Food color: School colors, Leaf Green

REVIEW TECHNIQUES

Roses
Leaves and stems
Writing
Reverse scroll border
Shell border

INSTRUCTIONS

1. At least 1 day in advance, make 6 tip 104 roses. Or, use Buttercream Icing and make roses and place on cake with scissors.
2. Ice cake on foil-covered board.
3. Pipe a tip 32 bottom shell border. Pipe a tip 16 top reverse scroll border.

4. Pipe tip 2 stems on top of cake. Add tip 350 leaves. Position roses on stems. Pipe tip 104 rosebuds.
5. Pipe tip 2 message on top of cake. Place diploma and hat as shown.

Wedding and Anniversary Cakes

Following are helpful tips to make decorating a wedding cake as simple as decorating any small cake.

- When making a cake mix in very warm weather, use cold water and eggs.
- To obtain uniform batter, scrape the bottom and sides of the mixing bowl often.
- Fill the baking pan only half full with batter.
- For a tall cake, bake 3 layers in 2-inch-deep pans rather than deeper pans.
- Crumb coat the cake as soon as it cools to help retain moistness.
- For a balanced look there should be at least a 2-inch difference in size between each layer. Each tier should be the same height or uniformly taller than the layer above it.
- To help bake a level cake and keep the edges from becoming too brown, cut strips of sheeting and fold several times to the depth of the cake pan. Moisten the cloth thoroughly and pin it securely to the outside of the pan. Commercial reusable cake strips are available for this purpose also.

- Buttercream Icing is best to use to keep the cake moist. For more well defined borders and string work, use Boiled Icing.
- For the whitest icing, use clear vanilla and water rather than brown vanilla and milk.
- To keep the cake from sticking to the plate after being lifted, sprinkle coconut over the portion that the separator will rest on.
- When deciding on the type of decoration to be used, keep in mind that the heavier-looking decorations are best used on the bottom tiers with lighter, more delicate decorations on the upper tiers.

Cake Separators

There are many attractive separators available for use in making wedding cakes. When choosing the separator, be certain that it is heavy enough to withstand warping and that it provides adequate support.

Following is a description and directions for assembling the separators used in this book.

Country Kitchen Cake Stand

This set accomodates 6, 8, 10, 12, 14, and 16-inch cakes. Each layer rests on a translucent plate the same size as the cake. The translucent plate is molded with a 1-inch elevation which is iced to give the illusion of greater height. Legs are 1½, 5, 8, and 10 inches tall. The white base plates are 6, 8, 10, 12, and 14 inches wide.

How to assemble

1. Place each cake on its appropriate translucent plate. Ice the cake and the 1-inch elevation of the plate.
2. Insert the legs into the white base plate. Use 10-inch legs for tall pillars, 8-inch legs for short pillars, or 5-inch legs for a stacked cake.
3. Insert the legs with the attached plate into the cake until the legs rest upon the translucent plate.
4. To complete assembly, place the translucent plate and cake over the appropriate white base plate.

Bush Separators for Stacked Cakes

Bush flat plates are 6, 8, 10, 12, and 14 inches wide. Each plate is used with 4 pegs which snap into the plate. For added support, use dowels as for above plates.

How to assemble

1. Place the bottom tier on a serving tray or foil-covered board and remaining tiers on respective flat plates. Ice all tiers.
2. Insert dowels cut to height into the bottom tier.
3. Insert pegs into the plate holding the second tier. Insert the pegs into the bottom tier.
4. Repeat procedure for remaining tiers and decorate.

Wilton Crystal Leg Stand

This set is elegant, yet sturdy. The plates are 6, 8, 10, 12, 14, and 16 inches wide. The 7½-inch legs snap into the bottoms of the plates. To use for a stacked cake, simply saw the legs to the height of the cake so that when inserted through the cake they do not show.

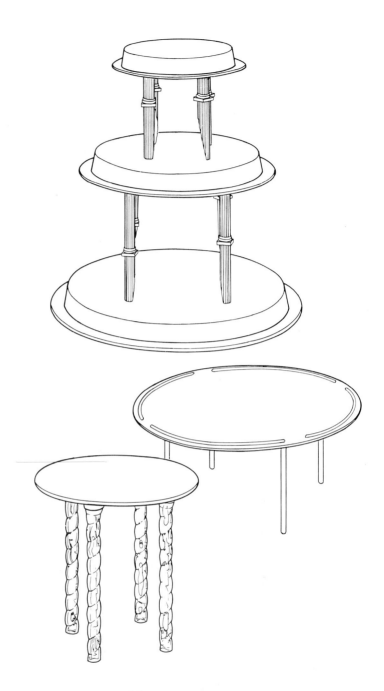

How to assemble

1. Place the largest tier on a serving tray or foil-covered board and ice. Place remaining tiers on plates at least ½ inch larger than the cake and ice.
2. Lightly mark all but the top tier to show where the legs will be inserted, being certain that each is centered. Use a plate without legs as a guide. Attach legs to plates. If making a stacked cake, stack all tiers and decorate. If making a pillared cake, do not assemble until cake is delivered.

Bush and Wilton Cake Stands

These sets have two plates and four pillars to separate each tier. Four pegs snap into each plate; these pegs are inserted into the tiers for support. Wilton plates are available in sizes from 6 through 18 inches; Bush plates are 6 through 14 inches. When choosing the size plate needed, choose those ½ inch wider than the cake to allow for border work. For added support, dowel rods can be cut to the height of the cake and inserted into the cake next to the pegs of the plate.

How to assemble

1. Place the bottom tier on a serving plate or foil-covered board and ice. Place remaining tiers on respective plates. Ice and decorate all tiers.
2. Insert dowel rods into all but the top tier.
3. Insert pegs into plates.
4. Secure pillars to studs.

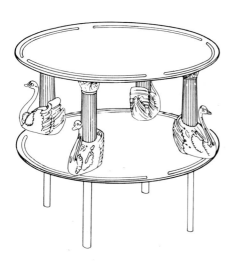

WEDDING CAKE CHART

The chart below is for smaller wedding-size pieces of cake. If making a cake for another occasion, plan on fewer servings per cake. The amounts of batter for pans is for cakes using whole eggs. If using egg whites only, add a little more batter to each pan.

PAN SIZE (inches)	APPROXIMATE SERVINGS	AMOUNT OF BATTER PER PAN (1 cake mix yields about 5 cups)	BAKING TIME
Round Pan (2 layers)			
6 x 2	10	½ cup	28-38 min.
8 x 2	16	2½ cups (½ pkg. mix)	25-35 min.
10 x 2	36	4 cups	35-45 min.
12 x 2	46	6 cups	35-45 min.
14 x 2	76	7½ cups (1½ pkg. mix)	40-50 min.
16 x 2	92	10 cups (2 pkg. mix)	45-55 min.
18 x 2	120	15 cups (3 pkg. mix)	50-60 min.
Rectangular Pan (1 layer)			
12 x 18 x 2	36-40	10 cups (2 pkg. mix)	40-50 min.

Figure Piped Bride and Groom, 36
Pink Roses Cake, 37

Figure Piped Bride and Groom Cake

Makes 60 servings

See photo on page 35

DECORATING NEEDS

2 recipes Royal Icing (½ cup Yellow, 1½ cups Pink, remaining divided and colored as directed under How to Figure Pipe Bride and Groom)

Cakes: 6, 8, 12 inches

Cake Separators: Wilton Crystal Leg set

White plates: 6 and 8 inches

Crystal legs: 8 7½-inch crystal legs (4 cut to cake height)

14" foil-covered board

5 recipes Buttercream Icing (2 cups Avocado, ½ cup Pink, remaining White

Food color: Cherry Pink, Lemon Yellow, Avocado, Black

Flower Nail #2

Waxed paper

Tips 1, 2, 4, 16, 101, 350, 101s

Top ornament

Silk flower spray, optional

REVIEW TECHNIQUES

Blossoms

Reverse scroll border

Hearts

Strings

Leaves

Assembling Wedding Cakes

INSTRUCTIONS

---

1. At least 1 day in advance, figure pipe 18 brides and grooms and 150 flower blossoms with Royal Icing.

2. Assemble cakes and plates as described on pages 33 and 34.

3. Pipe a tip 16 top and bottom reverse scroll border on each cake.

4. Attach the figure piped brides and grooms to the sides of the cakes with icing.

5. Pipe tip 2 strings and tip 4 hearts around the side of the cake.

6. Attach blossom arrangements with tip 350 leaves.

7. Place silk flower spray on middle cake, if desired.

8. Assemble cake as described on pages 33 and 34. Place desired ornament on top of cake. Pipe tip 2 strings to hang from the 6-inch cake if desired.

HOW TO FIGURE PIPE BRIDE AND GROOM

DECORATING NEEDS

Tips 2, 4, 6, 101s

Royal Icing Heads

Food Color: Black, White, Avocado, Pink, Yellow

Step 1 *Groom's Body* Pipe body with tip 6, beginning at the neck and increasing pressure slightly to form body.

Step 2 *Arm and Feet* Insert tip 6 into the left side of the body. Apply pressure moving the tip downward to form the leg and increasing pressure at the bottom to form the foot. Repeat for the other leg. Pipe the left arm beginning at the elbow, inserting the tip into the left shoulder.

Step 3 *Shoe, Shirt* Pipe dots at the bottom of the feet for shoes. Pipe a dot at the neck to secure Royal Icing head. Pipe a tip 6 white shirt.

Step 4 *Lapel, Coat, Bow Tie, Head, Bride's Dress* Outline the lapel and pipe a line to separate the pants from the coat. Pipe a bow tie at the neck. Press a Royal Icing head onto the neck. Pipe a tip 6 neck and bodice for the bride. Pipe tip 101s ruffles to finish the dress.

Step 5 *Bride's Arm, Hair, Flowers* Pipe bride's arm with tip 6. Pipe bride's hair with tip 2. Pipe tip 4 flower spray with tip 2 centers.

Pink Roses Cake

Makes 250 servings

See photo on page 35

DECORATING NEEDS

1½ recipes Royal Icing (4½ cups Pink, 1 cup Mulberry)
Cakes: 6, 10, 14, 18 inches
Cake separators: Country Kitchen
Translucent plates: 6, 10, 14 inches
White base plates: 6, 10, 14 inches
Legs: 5, 8, 10 inches
Country Kitchen clear plastic serving tray
11 recipes Buttercream Icing (3 cups Leaf Green, remainder White)
Tips 4, 6, 32, 104, 224, 352
Cake top
Ceramic bride and groom figures
1 spray silk flowers
Food color: Pink, Mulberry, Leaf Green
Gold Metallic leaves (optional)

REVIEW TECHNIQUES

Roses
Dots
Drop flowers
Shell border
Strings
Hearts
Scroll border
Leaves and stems
Assembling Wedding Cakes

INSTRUCTIONS
---

1. At least 1 day in advance, make 70 tip 104 roses and 200 tip 224 drop flowers with tip 4 centers with Royal Icing.
2. Place the 6, 10, and 14-inch cakes on the translucent plates and ice with white buttercream icing. Place the 18-inch cake on the serving plate and ice. Stack the 14-inch cake on the 18-inch cake using the 5-inch legs and 14-inch white base plates for support. (See pages 33 and 34 for specific instructions.)
3. Pipe a tip 32 bottom shell border on each cake. Pipe a tip 32 reverse scroll border around

top of each cake. Pipe tip 4 strings near the top and toward the bottom of each cake. Pipe tip 6 hearts, dots, and swans between rows of strings.
4. Arrange flowers as shown, attaching with tip 352 leaves. Push gold metallic leaves into arrangements if desired. Put silk flower spray on 10-inch cake.
5. Place bride and groom on 14-inch cake. Assemble cake with legs and white base plates as described on pages 33 and 34. Place desired ornament on top of cake.

Overleaf:
Peach Daisy Cake, 41

Blue Rose Cake, 40
Yellow Rose Cake, 41

Blue Rose Cake

Makes 270 servings

See photo on pages 38 and 39

DECORATING NEEDS

Plastic molds: church, bride and groom
Candy coating: 1 pound white, ½ pound blue,
  2 wafers *each* color: peach, brown,
  yellow, green, orchid
1 recipe Royal Icing (Blue)
Cakes: 8-inch, 2 12-inch, 2 16-inch
Separators: Country Kitchen
Clear plastic plates: 1 8-inch, 2 12-inch
White base plates: 1 8-inch, 2 12-inch
Legs: 8 5-inch, 4 10-inch
Base: 24 x 36-inch foil-covered board
13 recipes Buttercream Icing (1 cup Mint Green,
  remaining White)
Silk flower spray
Food color: Royal Blue, Mint Green
Tips 2, 16, 32, 103, 350
Cake top
Gold metallic leaves

REVIEW TECHNIQUES

Roses
Chocolate molding
Reverse scroll border
Shell border
Strings
Assembling Wedding Cakes

INSTRUCTIONS

1. At least 1 day in advance, make 68 tip 103 roses with Royal Icing. Mold chocolate church and figures.

2. Place the 16-inch cakes on the foil-covered board and ice. Place the 12-inch cakes on the 12-inch translucent plates. Push the 5-inch legs into the 12-inch white base plates. Push the legs and plates into the 16-inch cakes, centering carefully. Place the 12-inch cakes on top of the 16-inch cakes, using 5-inch legs and 12-inch white plate for support.

3. Place the 8-inch cake on the 8-inch translucent plate.

4. Push 10-inch legs with 8-inch white plate into 16-inch cakes as shown.

5. Ice all cakes.

6. Pipe a bottom tip 32 shell border around all cakes. Pipe a tip 32 top vertical shell border around the sides of all cakes. Pipe tip 2 strings from vertical shells. Pipe a tip 16 reverse scroll border around tops of cakes.

7. Place church in center of right tier. Place bride and groom figures in front of church, securing on a candy wafer with a little warmed candy coating to stand. Place the flower spray in the center of the left tier.

8. Pipe a tip 350 line cascading down front of each cake with mint green icing. Attach roses to wet icing. Push in metallic leaves. Pipe tip 350 leaves around roses.

9. When cake is delivered, complete assembly by placing the 8-inch translucent plate over the 8-inch white base plate. Tip 2 strings may be hung from 8-inch cake if desired.

10. Place desired ornament on top of cake.

Yellow Rose Cake

Makes 150 servings

See photo on page 39

DECORATING NEEDS

½ recipe Flower Decorator or Royal Icing (Yellow)
Cakes: 6, 8, 12, 16 inches
Bush flat plates: 6, 8, 12 inch
12 Bush pegs and extra dowel rods
Country Kitchen clear plastic crystal tray
9 recipes Buttercream Icing, (1 cup Green,
    remainder White)
Flower Nail #7
Food Color: Lemon Yellow, Leaf Green
Tips 2, 32, 88, 104, 352

REVIEW TECHNIQUES

Roses
Star border
Strings
Reverse scroll border
Stems and leaves
Wiggle swags
Assembling Wedding Cakes

—————————————— INSTRUCTIONS ——————————————

1. At least 1 day in advance, make 16 tip 104 roses and 8 rosebuds with Flower Decorator or Royal Icing.
2. Place the 6-, 8-, and 12-inch cakes on their respective flat plates and ice. Place the 16-inch cake on the plastic tray and ice.
3. Stack cakes, placing the back of each layer flush with the layer it rests upon to make steps, using the dowel rods and pegs for support.
4. Pipe a tip 32 bottom star border around each cake.
5. Pipe a tip 88 wiggle border around sides of each cake. Pipe tip 2 strings over wiggle borders.

6. Pipe a tip 16 top reverse scroll border around each cake.
7. Place the ribbon down the center of the cake, securing with dots of icing.
8. Pipe tip 2 stems on each tier.
9. Attach roses with dots of icing. Pipe tip 352 leaves around roses.
10. Place desired ornament on top of cake.
Note: If transporting cake, slide a heavy board under the plastic tray before moving to avoid cracking the plastic plate.

Peach Daisy Cake

Makes 150 servings

See photo on page 38

DECORATING NEEDS

1 recipe Royal Icing (1 cup Peach)*
Cakes: 6, 8, 12, 16 inches
Cake separators: Country Kitchen
Clear plastic plates: 6, 8, 12 inches
White base plates: 6, 8, 12 inches
Legs: 4 10-inch, 8 5-inch
Country Kitchen clear plastic crystal tray
10 recipes Buttercream Icing (2 cups Green,
    4 cups Peach, remaining Light Peach)
Food color: Leaf Green, Cherry Pink, Lemon Yellow
Tips 2, 4, 16, 32, 104, 224, 352
Cake top

REVIEW TECHNIQUES

Daisies
Drop flowers
Shell border
Reverse scroll border
Stems and leaves
Assembling Wedding Cakes

*To color icing peach, first color with Cherry Pink food color until light pink, then add Lemon Yellow, a little at a time, until desired shade of peach is achieved. The cake is iced in light peach. Flowers and borders are a darker shade of peach.

1. At least 1 day in advance, make 200 tip 104 white daisies with tip 4 peach centers. Make peach drop flowers with tip 224 and tip 2 white centers.

2. Place the 16-inch cake on the plastic serving tray and ice. Place the 12-inch cake on the 12-inch clear plastic plate. Stack the 12-inch cake on the 16-inch cake and ice. Use the 12-inch white base plate and 5-inch legs for support. Place the 8-inch cake on the 8-inch clear plastic plate; ice the cake and lip of the plate. Place the 6-inch cake on the 6-inch clear plastic plate. Center the 6-inch cake on the 8-inch cake and stack using 5-inch legs and 8-inch white base plate for support. Ice the 6-inch cake.

3. Pipe a tip 32 bottom shell border on each cake.

4. Pipe a tip 16 top reverse scroll border on each cake.

5. Pipe a tip 2 flowing stem line around the center of each cake.

6. Attach daisies and drop flower arrangements with tip 352 leaves.

7. Attach the 10-inch legs to the white 8-inch base plate. Push the legs into the 12-inch cake, being certain to center legs. Part of the legs will show and serve as pillars. Place the 8- and 6-inch cakes on the white plate.

8. Place desired ornament on top of cake.

Silver Anniversary

Makes 120 servings

See photo on opposite page

DECORATING NEEDS

1 recipe Royal Icing (Pink)
Cakes: 6, 8, 10, 14 inches
Base: 16-inch board covered with silver foil
Bush separators: 2 6-inch studded plates, 2 8-inch studded plates, 1 10-inch flat plate, 12 pegs
Silver metallic pillars: 4 3-inch, 4 5-inch
Dowel rods
10 recipes Buttercream Icing (2 cups Green, remainder White)
Food color: Cherry Pink, Leaf Green
Flower Nail #7
Tips 2, 16, 32, 102, 350

Silver metallic leaves and bells
Plastic figure (silver)
Cake top

REVIEW TECHNIQUES

Roses
Stems and leaves
Shell border
Reverse scroll border
Wiggle border
Wiggle swag
Strings
Assembling Wedding Cakes

1. At least 1 day in advance, make 70 tip 102 roses.

2. Slide the 14-inch cake onto the foil-covered board and ice. Place the 10-inch cake on the 10-inch flat plate and stack on the 14-inch cake with dowel rods and pegs, centering carefully. Place the 8-inch cake on the 8-inch plate; the 6-inch cake on the 6-inch plate. Ice both cakes. Insert pegs into the remaining 8- and 6-inch plates. Push pegs and plates into 8- and 10-inch cakes with the studs up.

3. Pipe a tip 32 bottom shell border around each cake.

4. Pipe a tip 16 scroll border around top of each cake.

5. Pipe tip 16 wiggle border around the plastic plates on the 8-inch and 10-inch cakes.

6. Pipe tip 16 wiggle swags around sides of each cake. Pipe tip 2 strings over each swag.

7. Arrange roses on cakes, attaching with tip 350 leaves. Press metallic leaves among roses.

8. Attach the bride and groom with a little icing as shown. Place bells on 8-inch layer; attach with icing.

9. Place the pillars on the studs and assemble the cake. Hang strings with tip 2 from 6" and 8" cakes if desired.

10. Place desired ornament on top of cake.

Golden Anniversary

Makes about 50 serving

See photo on page 42

DECORATING NEEDS

1 recipe Royal Icing (Gold)
Cakes: 6 and 12 inches
Cake separators: Country Kitchen
Clear plastic plate: 6-inch
White base plate: 6-inch
White legs: 4 8-inch
Base: 16-inch board covered with gold foil
4 recipes Buttercream Icing (2 cups Green, 3 cups White, remaining Light Gold)
1 recipe Royal Icing (Gold)
Flower Nail #7
Tips 2, 16, 32, 103, 350
Food color: Gold, Leaf Green
Gold metallic leaves
Foil numeral
Top ornament

REVIEW TECHNIQUES

Roses and rosebuds
Shell border
Strings
Reverse scroll border
Stems and leaves
Assembling Wedding Cakes

INSTRUCTIONS

Cake is iced in light gold icing, with white borders.

1. At least 1 day in advance, make 35 tip 103 roses and 35 rosebuds with Royal Icing.

2. Place the 6-inch cake on the 6-inch clear plastic plate and ice.

3. Place the 12-inch cake on the foil-covered board and ice.

4. Pipe a tip 32 bottom shell border around each cake.

5. Pipe a tip 16 shell border about ¾ inch above bottom border on each cake. Pipe tip 16 strings around top of each cake. Pipe a tip 16 reverse scroll border around the top of each cake.

6. Pipe a tip 2 flowing stem line around the side of each cake. Add tip 352 leaves. Attach prepared rosebuds with icing.

7. Push the foil numeral into the center of the 12-inch cake, securing with a little icing.

8. Arrange roses on cakes. Pipe tip 352 leaves around roses. Push metallic leaves among arrangements.

9. Pipe tip 2 stems and tip 352 leaves in four equally spaced positions on sides of bottom cake. Attach a rose in the center of each.

10. Push the separator legs into the white 6-inch plate. Push the legs with the white base plate into the 12-inch cake. Part of the legs will show and serve as pillars. Place the 6-inch cake on the white plate.

11. Place desired ornament on top of cake.

Holiday Cakes

Four Leaf Clover

See photo on page 46

DECORATING NEEDS

8-, 9-, or 10-inch layer cake
Foil-covered board (2 inches larger than cake)
1 recipe Buttercream Icing (White)
Colored gumdrops
Clear piping gel
1½-inch artist brush
Green decorating sugar
Tip 1

REVIEW TECHNIQUES

Writing

INSTRUCTIONS
---

1. Bake desired size cake. Ice cake on foil-covered board.
2. Stand gumdrops in a circle around base of cake while icing is still soft.
3. Using pattern as a guide, draw a four-leaf clover to fit the cake. To make the pattern, trace baking pan on a large sheet of paper. Cut out circle and fold in fourths. Cut in the shape of a single clover leaf. (Fig. 1) Unfold paper to make whole shamrock pattern.
4. When crust forms on icing, place pattern lightly on top of cake. Use a toothpick to outline the pattern. Draw a stem with the toothpick.
5. Use the brush to moisten the inside of the clover with clear piping gel.
6. Sprinkle inside of shamrock with green sugar to cover completely.
7. Pipe tip 1 message on top of cake.

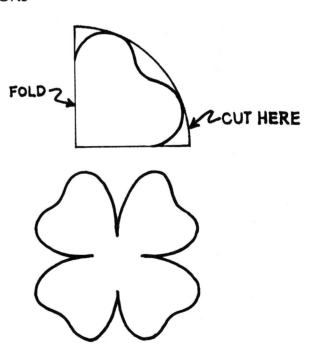

FOLD

CUT HERE

Be My Valentine

See photo on page 46

DECORATING NEEDS

9-inch heart cake
12-inch foil-covered board
½ recipe Royal Icing (½ cup Cherry Pink, remainder Royal Red)
2 recipes Buttercream Icing (3 cups Red, 1 cup Leaf Green, remainder Pink)
Tips 2, 3, 4, 16, 102, 350
Flower Nail #7
Food color: Cherry Pink, Royal Red, Leaf Green

REVIEW TECHNIQUES

Shell border
Reverse scroll border
Run sugar
Hearts
Roses and rosebuds
Stems and leaves

INSTRUCTIONS

---

1. At least 1 day in advance, make the run sugar heart with Royal Icing as listed.
2. Ice the cake on the foil-covered board with pink icing.
3. Pipe a tip 16 red top reverse scroll border. Pipe a tip 16 bottom shell border. Pipe tip 4 hearts around sides of cake.
4. Place the run sugar heart on top of the cake.

Pipe a tip 3 shell border around the edge of run sugar heart.
5. Pipe tip 2 green stems and tip 350 leaves on the run sugar heart.
6. Make a tip 104 rose with pink icing. Lift rose off flower nail with shears and place on heart.
7. Pipe a tip 104 rosebud directly on the heart.

Be My Valentine, this page
Four Leaf Clover, 45

Spring is Here!

See photo on page 51

DECORATING NEEDS

10-inch layer cake
12-inch foil-covered board
2½ recipes Buttercream Icing (¼ cup Pink, ½ cup Grey [made with a little Black], ⅛ cup Green, ⅛ cup Black, ⅛ cup Brown, 1 cup Chartreuse, remainder White)
Food color: Chartreuse, Pink, Black, Leaf Green, Brown
Tips 1, 2, 4, 16, 32, 224, 320, 350

REVIEW TECHNIQUES

Stencils
Drop flowers
Star flowers
Stems
Dots
Shell border
Wiggle border
Strings

INSTRUCTIONS

1. Ice cake on foil-covered board. Let stand about 20 minutes or until icing forms a crust.
2. Make stencils using patterns below.
3. Position stencils on top of cake as shown. Ice rabbit with grey icing; sprinkling can with pink icing. Lift stencil from cake.
4. Pipe tip 4 brown branches rising from sprinkling can. Pipe tip 320 chartreuse star flowers on branches.
5. Pipe tip 2 dots on sprinkling can.
6. Pipe tip 224 grey drop flowers with tip 2 centers near top of sprinkling can.
7. Pipe tip 350 leaves around drop flowers on sprinkling can.
8. Outline rabbit with tip 1. Make tip 2 eyes with tip 1 centers. Pipe a strip of pink icing on each ear and a dot for the nose with tip 2.
9. Pipe a tip 32 bottom shell border. Pipe tip 320 star flowers in pairs evenly around base of cake on top of shell border. Pipe a tip 16 wiggle border.
10. Pipe tip 16 strings from top of cake.

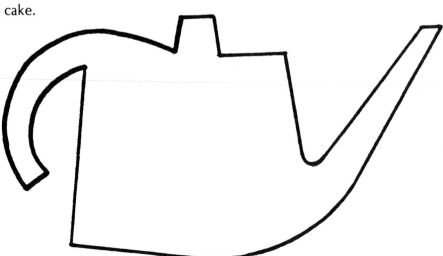

Easter Happiness

See photo on page 51

DECORATING NEEDS

10-inch layer cake
12-inch foil-covered board
**2 recipes Buttercream Icing (2 cups Leaf Green,
    remainder White)**
½ recipe Royal Icing (White)
½ recipe Royal Icing (Black, Mulberry, Royal Blue, White)
Waxed paper
Piping gel
Food color: Mulberry, Royal Blue, Black, Leaf Green
Flower nail #12
Tips 2, 16, 32, 88, 352
Artificial stamens

REVIEW TECHNIQUES

Easter Lilies
Stems and leaves
Wiggle swag border
Strings
Run sugar
Reverse scroll border
Shell border

INSTRUCTIONS

---

1. At least one day in advance, make the run sugar butterfly with Royal Icing as listed. Make 5 Easter Lilies with white Royal Icing, using artificial stamens for centers.

2. Ice cake on foil-covered board.

3. Pipe a tip 32 bottom shell border. Pipe a tip 88 wiggle swag border around the side of the cake. Pipe tip 2 strings over wiggle border. Pipe a tip 16 top reverse scroll border.

4. Pipe tip 2 stems and tip 352 leaves on top of cake. Position Easter Lilies as shown, securing each with dots of icing.

5. Pipe butterfly body and head with tip 2. Stand run sugar wings in icing, securing with black royal icing. Support wings with a large tip until icing dries.

6. Pipe tip 2 dots around inside edge of top border.

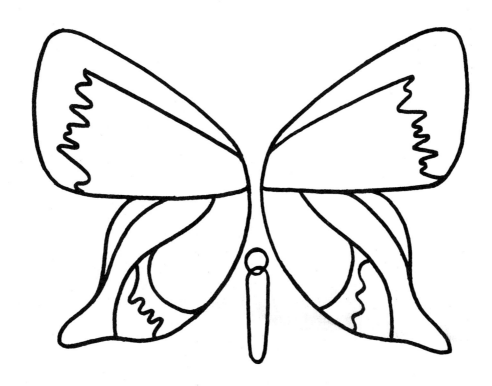

49

Easter Wishes

See photo on page 51

DECORATING NEEDS

8-inch layer cake
10-inch foil-covered board
½ recipe Royal Icing (Lemon Yellow)
2 recipes Buttercream Icing (2 cups Leaf Green, remainder White)
Food color: Lemon Yellow, Leaf Green
Tips 1, 2, 3, 16, 350, 352
Flower Nail #7

REVIEW TECHNIQUES

Jonquils
Bulb and drop border
Wiggle border
Star border

--- **INSTRUCTIONS** ---

1. At least 1 day in advance, make 7 tip 352 jonquils with tips 3 and 1 centers. Or, dry in oven at 100° F. for 30 minutes.
2. Ice cake on foil-covered board.
3. Pipe a tip 16 bottom star border. Pipe a tip 2 bulb and drop border and tip 2 top wiggle border.

4. Pipe tip 2 stems. Place jonquils on top of cake, attaching with dots of icing. Pipe tip 350 long leaves.
5. Pipe tip 1 message on top of cake.

Santa and His Elves

See photo on page 54

DECORATING NEEDS

8-inch layer cake
10-inch foil-covered board
3 recipes Royal Icing (Leaf Green, Lemon Yellow, Royal Red, Coppertone, Black, Gold, White)
2 recipes Buttercream Icing (1 cup Yellow, 1 cup Green, ½ cup Red, remainder White)
Food color: Lemon Yellow, Leaf Green, Royal Red, Coppertone, Black, Gold)
Tips 1, 2, 6, 16, 32, 101s, 350
Toothpicks

REVIEW TECHNIQUES

Shell border
Reverse scroll border
Leaves
Dots

--- **INSTRUCTIONS** ---

1. At least 1 day in advance, figure pipe Santa, Angel, and Elves.
2. At least 1 day in advance, make Christmas tree, following directions on page 59.
3. Ice cake on foil-covered board.
4. Pipe a tip 32 bottom shell border. Pipe a tip 16 reverse scroll border around top of cake.
5. Pipe a tip 2 flowing stem line around the side of the cake. Pipe tip 352 leaves over the stems, using a toothpick to pull out points as they are made. Pipe tip 2 dots for holly berries.

6. Stand the tree in the center of the cake.
7. Use a small amount of Royal Icing to secure the angel to the top of the tree.
8. Pipe white dots in a circle around the tree to stand Santa and elf figures in. Stand figures on top of cake. Let stand about 1 hour before moving the cake.

HOW TO
FIGURE PIPE SANTA CLAUS

DECORATING NEEDS

½ recipe Royal Icing (as listed in main ingredients)
Tips 2, 6
Fine artist brush

Step 1 *Head* Pipe head with tip 2 in a bag of flesh-colored (coppertone) icing. Hold tip perpendicular to and ⅛ inch above surface. Apply pressure to form a ball.

Step 2 *Cheeks and Nose* Insert tip 2 into one side of ball and move in a circle while applying light pressure, keeping tip under surface of icing. Repeat for the other cheek. Pipe a small dot in the center for a nose.

Step 3 *Hat, Body, Legs* Use tip 6 to form hat. Hold bag at a 45° angle and apply heavy pressure close to the head, decreasing pressure as tip is pulled away to form a point. To make body, hold tip at a 45° angle at the neck and apply light pressure. Move tip down, increasing pressure to form stomach. Release pressure and pull tip away. To make legs, insert tip 6 into one side of body at the bottom at a 45° angle. Apply pressure while moving tip away from body, increasing pressure to make feet. Release pressure and pull away. Repeat for the other leg.

Step 4 *Arms, Facial Features, Hat Trim, Pant Legs* Insert tip 6 into shoulder on one side at a 45° angle. Apply pressure, moving tip away from body to form arm. Repeat for the other arm. Use the artist brush and black and red paste colors thinned with a little water to paint eyes and mouth on the face. Use tip 2 to pipe on beard, mustache, and eyebrows. Use tip 2 to form a ball at the end of hat. Pipe ball at ends of legs.

Step 5 *Boots, Mittens, Jacket Trim* Use tip 2 to pipe balls on each foot for boots. Pipe balls at ends of arms and coat trim.

Step 6 Pipe tip 2 green mittens on ends of arms.

HOW TO
FIGURE PIPE ANGELS

DECORATING NEEDS

1 Royal Icing head
½ recipe Royal Icing (as listed in main ingredients)
Tips 1, 101s

Step 1   *Gown*   Pipe tip 101s bottom ruffle of gown, touching the surface with the wide end and moving slightly up and down to form ruffle. Pipe second row of ruffles, making it a little shorter than bottom row and slightly overlapping. Pipe a third row of ruffles, a little shorter than the second row and slightly overlapping.

Step 2   *Neck and head*   Pipe a small amount of icing at the top center, attached to the gown. Press Royal Icing head onto neck.

Step 3   *Hair, Wings, Halo*   Pipe tip 1 hair, wings, and halo. If desired, halo can be sprinkled with glitter. To do so, allow hair and wings to dry before piping on halo; then sprinkle with glitter.

HOW TO
FIGURE PIPE ELVES

DECORATING NEEDS

Royal Icing as listed in main ingredients
Tips 1, 2
Fine artist brush
Black paste color

Note: Finished elves should be about two-thirds the size of Santa Claus.

Step 1   *Head*   Follow directions as in **Step 1 (How to Figure Pipe Santa Claus)**, making head smaller. Use tip 2 to make elongated eyes toward the left side of the face.

Step 2   *Eyes, Nose, Ear, Body, Arms*   Use the artist brush to paint a dot of black paste color on lower part of each eye. Use tip 2 to pipe an ear on the right side of the head. Pipe a small nose at the base of the eyes, holding the tip perpendicular to the face and applying pressure to attach the nose, decreasing pressure as tip is pulled away. To make body and arms, follow directions as in **Step 3 (How to Figure Pipe Santa Claus).**

Step 3   *Hat, Arms, Base of Body, Legs and Feet*   Use tip 2 to form hands by making a small ball at the end of each arm. To make thumb and fingers, insert tip into ball, apply pressure and pull out. To make the hat, use tip 2 and red

icing. Hold the bag at a 45° angle close to the top of head. Apply heavy pressure, move away to form a point, decreasing pressure as tip moves. Use tip 2 and green icing to form body and legs. Hold bag at a 45° angle at the base of the shirt and apply pressure, moving the tip along the bottom of the shirt from right to left. After completing body, move down to form left leg, increasing pressure to form a foot. Release pressure and break off. Repeat for the other leg. Use thinned pink paste color and the artist brush to paint on the mouth.

53

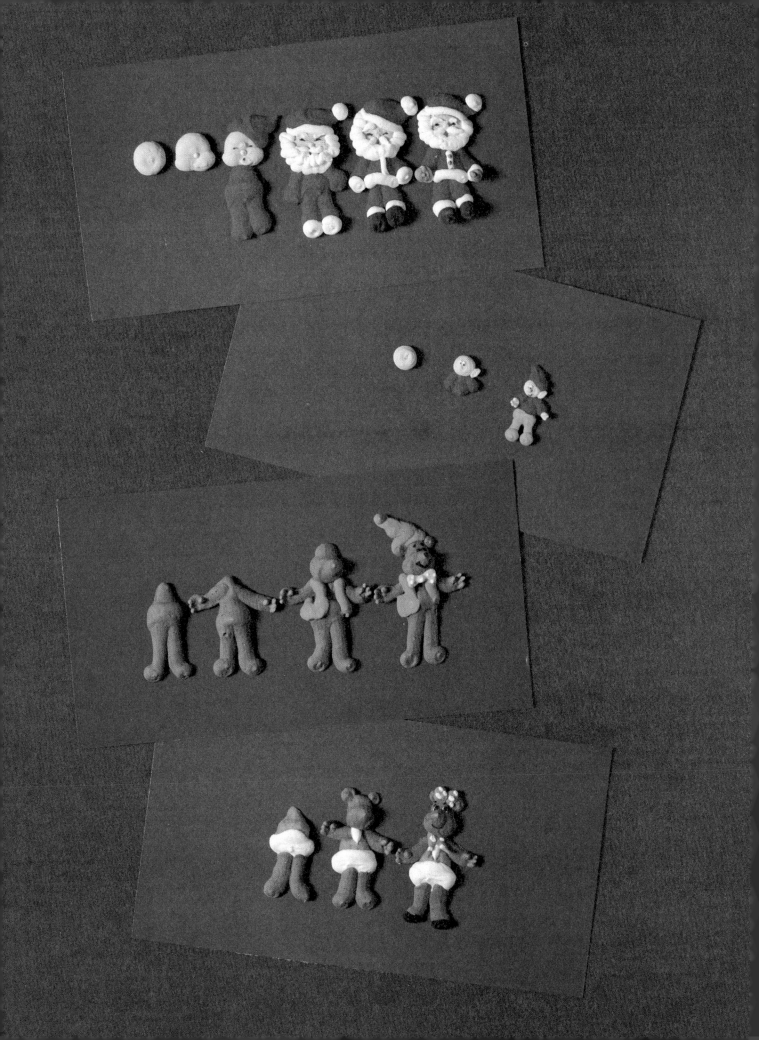

Ted E. Bear and Patti Bear

See photo on page 55

DECORATING NEEDS

8-inch layer cake
10-inch foil-covered board
4 recipes Buttercream Icing (Orange, Brown, Black,
   Royal Blue, Chartreuse, Royal Red, Leaf Green, White)
Food color: Orange, Brown, Black, Royal Blue,
   Chartreuse, Royal Red, Leaf Green
Tips 1, 2, 3, 6, 7, 16, 32, 350

REVIEW TECHNIQUES

Shell border
Leaves
Dots
Writing

INSTRUCTIONS

1. Ice cake on foil-covered board.
2. Pipe a tip 32 bottom shell border. Pipe a tip 16 top shell border.
3. Pipe tip 352 leaves in clusters around bottom and top borders. Pull out tips with a toothpick. Pipe tip 2 dots in clusters in leaves to resemble holly.
4. Pipe Ted. E. Bear and Patti Bear following directions below. Pipe Santa Claus following directions on page 52, using tips one size larger.

HOW TO FIGURE PIPE TED E. BEAR

DECORATING NEEDS

Food color: Brown, Chartreuse, Blue, Black
Tips 1, 2, 6

Step 1 *Body, Legs, Feet, Arms* Pipe body with tip 6 in brown icing, beginning at the neck and increasing pressure to form stomach. Without releasing pressure, move tip downward to form the right leg and foot, using slightly more pressure at the foot. Insert the tip into the left side of the body. Apply pressure, moving the tip down to form the left leg and foot. Insert tip into shoulder. Apply pressure to form an arm. Form fingers with tip 1.

Step 2 *Vest* Pipe a tip 2 vest and tie.

Step 3 *Head and Facial Features* Form the head with tip 6, holding the tip perpendicular to the surface. Apply light pressure and increase pressure to form cheeks. Move tip upward to form the nose. Make two dots for ears. Add facial features with tip 1.

HOW TO
FIGURE PIPE PATTI BEAR

DECORATING NEEDS

Food color: Orange, Brown, Black
Tips 1, 2, 6

Step 1 *Blouse and Skirt* Form the blouse with tip 6 and orange icing. Use tip 6 and white icing to form the skirt, making it fuller at the bottom by increasing pressure.

Step 2 *Legs, Feet, Arms* Use tip 6 to form as for Ted E. Bear. Form fingers with tip 1.

Step 3 *Vest and Ties* Use tip 2 to form vest. Make tip 2 ties. Trim with tip 1 white dots.

Step 4 *Head and Facial Features* Form head with tip 6, beginning with light pressure and increasing pressure to form cheeks. Move tip upward to form the nose. Make two dots for ears. Add tip 1 facial features.

Santa's On His Way

See photo on page 54

DECORATING NEEDS

Plastic molds: Trees, Santa Claus, and Deer
14-inch layer cake
16-inch foil-covered board
3 recipes Buttercream Icing (2 cups Red, remainder White)
Chocolate-flavored candy coating: ½ pound white, 1 pound chocolate, ½ pound red, 1 pound green wafers, ¼ pound butterscotch, 3 pink wafers
Edible white glitter
Food color: Christmas Red
Tips 2, 16, 32

REVIEW TECHNIQUES

Chocolate molding
Shell border
Writing

INSTRUCTIONS

1. At least 1 hour in advance, mold candy pieces.
2. Trim cake to level, reserving trimmings for step 6. Ice cake on foil-covered board.
3. Pipe a tip 32 shell border around the base and top of the cake.
4. Pipe tip 16 loop over shells in red icing.
5. Pipe tip 2 message on side of cake.

6. Sprinkle edible white glitter on top of cake. Stand chocolate pieces on top of cake. If desired, arrange cake trimmings on top of cake; ice and sprinkle with glitter. Press chocolate pieces into trimmings.
7. Stand chocolate pieces in snow as shown.

Christmas Wedding

Makes 100 servings

See photo on page 55

DECORATING NEEDS

Cakes: 6, 10, 14 inches
Cake separator: Wilton Crystal Clear Divider Set
Cake plates: 8, 10 inches
Legs: 8 twist
Base: 16-inch foil-covered board
1 recipe Royal Icing (½ cup Yellow, ½ cup Green, remaining Red)
Flower Nail #7
Waxed paper
8 recipes Buttercream Icing (2 cups Green, ½ cup Red, remainder White)

Food color: Royal Red, Emerald Green, Lemon Yellow
Tips 2, 3, 32, 352
Miniature bride and groom
Decorated Royal Icing Christmas Tree (below)
Toothpicks

REVIEW TECHNIQUES

Poinsettias
Leaves and stems
Shell border
Dots
Assembling wedding cakes (pages 33-34)

INSTRUCTIONS

1. At least 1 day in advance, make Royal Icing Christmas Tree.

2. At least 1 day in advance, make 32 tip 352 Royal Icing poinsettias with dot centers (use parchment bags with tiny holes cut in bottom) using Royal Icing as listed.

3. Place the 16-inch cake on the foil-covered board and ice. Saw 1 set of the twist legs to the height of the 16-inch cake. Push the shortened twist legs attached to the 10-inch plate. Push the shortened legs into the 16-inch cake so that only the plate is showing, being certain that the plate is centered.

4. Slide the 10-inch cake onto the 10-inch plate. Ice the cake.

5. Place the 6-inch cake on the 8-inch plate and ice.

6. Pipe a tip 32 top and bottom shell border on each cake.

7. Pipe a tip 2 flowing stem line around the side of each cake. Cover most of the line with tip 352 leaves in green icing. After each leaf is made, pull out points with a toothpick.

8. Pipe tip 3 red berries in arrangements around leaves.

9. Arrange poinsettias as shown, attaching with tip 352 leaves.

10. Push the twist legs into the 8-inch plate. Push the legs into the 10-inch cake, centering carefully.

11. Stand the Royal Icing tree on top along with the miniature bride and groom.

HOW TO MAKE A CHRISTMAS TREE

DECORATING NEEDS

1 recipe Royal Icing (½ cup Yellow, ½ cup Red, ½ cup White, remainder Green)
Tips 1, 352
Parchment triangles or plastic bags
Sugar cone or parchment triangle

Step 1 Use sugar cone for base of tree or make a cone from a parchment triangle. Stand cone on a sheet of waxed paper. Pipe a row of tip 352 leaves around the base of the cone. Pipe a second row of leaves above the first row, overlapping slightly. Repeat until cone is covered with leaves.

Step 2 Pipe tip 1 dots in strings over leaves to resemble popcorn.

Step 3 Make tip 1 bells by making a spiral. Pipe dots in centers for clappers.

Step 4 Pipe tip 1 balls with red trim.

Merry Christmas, 60
Wreath Bundt Cake, 63

Merry Christmas

See photo on page 58

DECORATING NEEDS

10-inch layer cake
14-inch foil-covered board
1 recipe Royal Icing (½ cup Red, ¼ cup Royal Blue,
½ cup Black, ½ cup Coppertone, remainder White)
Waxed paper
2 recipes Buttercream Icing (4 cups Royal Red, remainder
Emerald Green)
Food color: Royal Red, Emerald Green, Royal Blue, Black,
Coppertone
Tips 2, 4, 32

REVIEW TECHNIQUES

Shell border
Strings
Run sugar
Writing

--- INSTRUCTIONS ---

1. At least 1 day in advance, make the run sugar Santa face, outlining with tip 2 and black royal icing. Fill in with thinned icing as listed.
2. Ice cake on foil-covered board.

3. Pipe a tip 32 top and bottom shell border. Pipe tip 4 strings from shell.
4. Place run sugar piece in center of cake.
5. Pipe tip 2 message on top of cake.

Holiday Greetings

See photo on page 54

DECORATING NEEDS

10-inch layer cake
12-inch foil-covered board
Clear plastic wreath mold
Chocolate-flavored candy coating: ½ pound chocolate,
⅛ pound yellow, 10 red wafers, 20 green wafers
20 butterscotch wafers
3 recipes Buttercream Icing (2 cups Leaf Green,
½ cup Red)
Food color: Leaf Green, Christmas Red
Tips 3, 352
Toothpicks

REVIEW TECHNIQUES

Leaves
Dots
Chocolate molding

--- INSTRUCTIONS ---

1. Make chocolate wreath following general instructions on page 79.
2. Ice cake on foil-covered board.
3. Pipe tip 352 leaves around top and bottom borders, pulling each out with a toothpick to make points.

4. Pipe tip 3 berries among leaves.
5. Place candy wreath in the center of the cake.

Wreath Bundt Cake

See photo on page 58

DECORATING NEEDS

1 recipe two-layer cake
10-inch bundt pan
12-inch foil-covered board
1 recipe Buttercream Icing (Emerald Green)
Cinnamon candies
Bow

INSTRUCTIONS

1. Bake cake in Bundt pan. Cool in pan 15 minutes before turning out onto a wire rack to cool completely.
2. Ice cake on foil-covered board.
3. Use a knife to pull out sharp points on icing.

4. Press cinnamon candies lightly into icing to make berry clusters.
5. Tape plastic wrap to the back of the bow. Press bow lightly onto icing.

Halloween Ghosts

See photo on page 62

DECORATING NEEDS

10-inch layer cake
12-inch foil-covered board
1½ pounds white candy coating
¼ pound orange candy coating
12 green candy coating wafers
Black candy color
Three-dimensional ghost mold
Large three-dimensional ghost mold
Flat-back ghost mold
Artist brushes
Food color: Black, Orange
2 recipes Buttercream Icing (3 cups Black, remainder Orange)
Tips 4, 16, 32

REVIEW TECHNIQUES

Shell border
Dots
Star border
Chocolate painting and molding

INSTRUCTIONS

1. Make all candy molded pieces following samples in photo.
2. Ice cake on foil-covered board.
3. Pipe a tip 32 top star border and a bottom shell border.
4. Pipe a tip 16 shell border under star border.

5. Pipe tip 4 dots in center of each star.
6. Attach flat-backed molded candy to side of cake with dots of icing. Stand large ghost in center of cake. Press sucker mold sticks into cake around center ghost.

From top: The Witch is Out, 64
The Pumpkin Patch, 64
Halloween Ghosts, this page

The Pumpkin Patch

See photo on page 62

DECORATING NEEDS

10-inch layer cake
12-inch foil-covered board
1 recipe Royal Icing (½ cup Yellow, ½ cup Green, ½ cup Black, remainder Orange)
Waxed paper
Fine artist brush
2 recipes Buttercream Icing (2 cups Leaf Green)
Tips 2, 6, 32, 352

REVIEW TECHNIQUES

Star border
Leaves and stems
Run sugar

—————————— **INSTRUCTIONS** ——————————

1. At least 1 day in advance, make run sugar pumpkin, outlining with black and filling in with thinned colors as listed. When filling in leaves, allow orange and yellow icings to run together.
2. Ice cake on foil-covered board.
3. Pipe a tip 32 top and bottom star border.
4. Pipe 4 evenly spaced tip 6 pumpkins around base of cake. To make pumpkins, pipe a large dot on side of cake, then pipe heavy lines over the dot using heavy pressure. Pipe tip 2 stems on each pumpkin.
5. Pipe a tip 2 flowing stem from each pumpkin as shown.
6. Pipe tip 352 leaves over stem.
7. Place run sugar piece on top of cake.

The Witch Is Out

See photo on page 62

DECORATING NEEDS

12-inch layer cake
14-inch foil-covered board
1 recipe Royal Icing (½ cup Black, ½ cup Grey, ¼ cup Yellow, ¼ cup Coppertone)
Serrated knife
2 recipes Buttercream Icing (2 cups Black, remainder Orange)
Food color: Lemon Yellow, Coppertone, Orange, Black)
Tips 2, 12, 32

REVIEW TECHNIQUES

Run sugar
Shell border

—————————— **INSTRUCTIONS** ——————————

1. At least 1 day in advance make run sugar witch and broom end. Outline with black royal icing and fill in with thinned colors as listed.
2. Use a sharp serrated knife to cut a piece from cake to make a crescent-shaped moon.
3. Crumb coat cake with thinned Buttercream Icing. Let stand until icing forms a crust, then apply finishing coat of icing.
4. Pipe tip 32 top and bottom shell border. Place run sugar witch in center of cake.
5. Place a thin strip of poster-weight paper across the cake, positioning it so that the witch will "sit" on the broomstick. Pipe the broom handle over the paper with tip 12.
6. Carefully position run sugar witch over broom handle. Attach the broom end to the wet icing on the end of the broom handle.

Decorating Basics

Basic Equipment and Supplies

Decorating Bags These are cones made of disposable plastic, parchment, or reusable polyester-coated fabric that hold the decorating tip and are filled with icing. Disposable plastic bags are most useful when several colors of icing are called for. When large amounts of flowers or borders of the same color are needed, a reusable bag is best.

Parchment is sold in rolls or triangles and can be formed into a cone by following these directions:
Roll point B to meet point C to form a funnel. (Fig. 1) Roll point A to meet points B and C. (Fig. 2) The newly formed point D should be tight. Secure with tape. (Fig. 3)

To fill the decorating bag, insert decorating tip or coupler, if using, into bag. Turn top edge of bag over to form a cuff. Fill bag half full with icing. Unfold top of bag and press edges together. Fold down several times.

Decorating Tips These are open-ended, conical-shaped metal tips that are dropped through the decorating bag. Icing is forced through them to form various shapes. Tips range from a simple round opening to those that create special effects.

Couplers The use of a coupler enables you to change tips without changing decorating bags and to pipe more than one decoration in the same icing. Couplers can be used with plastic or parchment bags. To use a coupler follow these instructions:
1. **Remove the ring from the main part of the coupler.**
2. **Insert the coupler through the bag opening.**
3. **Trim bag so that four threads of the coupler are protruding.**
4. **Place the decorating tip over the end of the coupler. Secure by screwing the ring over the tip and onto the main part of the coupler.**

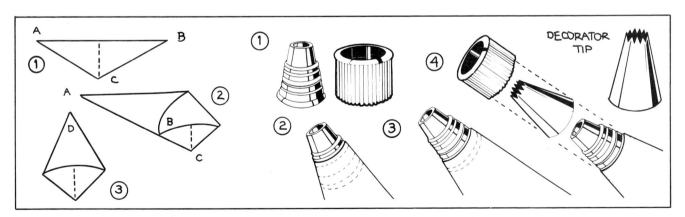

Food Color   Food color comes as paste, liquid paste, powder, or liquid. The first three forms are available at cake decorating supply outlets. These are concentrated and only small amounts are required. For best results, mix colors several hours before use, since they tend to darken over time. Always add food color a little at a time to achieve desired results. Basic beginning colors are red, yellow, blue, black, green, and brown.

Kitchen Equipment   A heavy-duty, free-standing mixer is best to use for icings since many of the decorator icings are too heavy for small hand mixers.

A good, solid turntable is useful in applying a smooth coating of icing on a cake. It also speeds border work by enabling you to move the turntable rather than the entire cake.

Use a wide blade spatula at least 12 inches long for the smoothest spreading. Smaller spatulas are also useful for special decorating needs. Spatulas are available in straight and offset blades.

Flower Nails   These are metal hand-held nails used to make various flowers. The most commonly used is the #7 nail.

Cake Boards, Foil, Doilies, and Separator Plates
These are all miscellaneous decorating accessories used to hold or enhance the finished cake. Cardboard should be at least 2 inches larger than the iced cake. Doilies should be the same size as the board and grease-resistant. Non-toxic, colorful foil or plastic can be used to cover the board before placing the cake on it.

Artist Brushes   Many techniques used in this book require a good quality fine line brush and a ½-inch brush.

Baking and Icing the Cake
A decorated cake is only as good as what is under the icing. For best results, keep these tips in mind when baking the cake.
- Preheat the oven according to the recipe instructions.
- Generously grease the inside of the cake pan. A grease and flour pan spray available in

supermarkets works well, as does a commercial pan grease available at cake decorating supply outlets.
- To help the cake bake evenly, use commercial baking strips, pinned securely around the sides of the pan.
- To prevent the batter from overflowing, fill the pans about half full with batter.
- Cool cakes in the pan on a wire rack 10 minutes before turning out onto a wire rack to cool completely.
- To remove cakes from pan, loosen edges with a knife. Place a cake rack across the top of the cake, and while holding securely, flip the cake and rack over.

Icings on the Cake
Important: prepare the cake for icing according to the following procedures:
- To ice a two-layer cake, trim cooled cake with a sharp knife to flatten layers. (Fig. 1)
- Spread the bottom layer with Buttercream Icing or filling. For best results, use a decorating turntable.
- Place trimmed sides of cake together. (Fig. 2)
- Use a long spatula to crumb ice the entire cake to seal in crumbs. Use only a small amount of icing. Let the cake stand at least 15 minutes or until icing forms a crust. (Fig. 3)
- Spread sides and top with a finish coat of icing. For a smooth finish, dip the spatula in boiling water for a few seconds, dry completely, and smooth icing. The hot spatula will melt the shortening in the icing and make it smooth.

Use these recipes as called for when decorating the cakes in this book.

Buttercream Icing

A good-flavored, rich icing used for frosting, borders, stars, leaves, stems, and many of the flowers.

½ cup vegetable shortening (High ratio shortening yields the lightest icing.)
1 teaspoon vanilla
½ teaspoon salt
½ teaspoon almond extract
¼ teaspoon butter flavoring
4 cups powdered sugar, sifted
5 tablespoons water

In a mixing bowl, cream shortening, vanilla, salt, and flavorings until smooth. Gradually beat in powdered sugar and water. Beat on low speed for 12 minutes.

Royal Icing

Makes lovely, well defined flowers, make-ahead decorations, and run sugar. An excellent commercial Royal Icing is available at cake decorating supply outlets.

⅔ cup water
¼ cup meringue powder*
½ teaspoon cream of tartar
8 cups (2 pounds) powdered sugar, sifted
1 tablespoon gum arabic*

In a mixing bowl, combine water, meringue powder, and cream of tartar; beat until stiff peaks form. Stir together powdered sugar and gum arabic. Gradually add powdered sugar mixture to meringue mixture, beating on low speed until stiff peaks form.

Flower Decorator Icing

Makes flowers that can be easily cut through when used on top of the cake. Because this icing contains a large amount of shortening, it is not palatable as an icing for the entire cake.

1 cup plus 2 tablespoons vegetable shortening (High ratio is best.)
1 egg white
½ teaspoon salt
½ teaspoon vanilla
4 cups (1 pound) powdered sugar, sifted

In a mixing bowl, combine shortening, egg white, salt, and vanilla. Gradually beat in half of the powdered sugar. Beat on low speed until well blended. Gradually beat in remaining powdered sugar; beat on low speed until smooth.

Boiled Icing

Use this icing for borders and string work.

½ cup meringue powder*
1 cup water
4 cups (1 pound) powdered sugar, sifted
¼ cup water
1 cup granulated sugar
¼ teaspoon cream of tartar

In a mixing bowl, beat meringue powder and 1 cup water on high speed until soft peaks form. Gradually beat in powdered sugar until smooth. Combine ¼ cup water, granulated sugar, and cream of tartar in a small saucepan. Cover and bring to a boil. Boil until steam rises from under cover. Remove cover and insert a candy thermometer. Boil until thermometer registers 250° F. Pour hot syrup over meringue mixture; beat until smooth.

Humid Weather Icing

Just as its name implies, this icing works well on damp days.

1½ cups vegetable shortening
1½ teaspoons vanilla
1 teaspoon butter flavoring
½ package (2½ tablespoons non-dairy dessert topping mix
¼ cup flour
¾ cup milk
8 cups (2 pounds) powdered sugar, sifted

In a mixing bowl, combine shortening, vanilla, butter flavoring, and dessert topping mix; blend well. Gradually blend in remaining ingredients; beat until smooth.

Egg White Royal Icing

Cannot be rewhipped.

3 large egg whites, room temperature
½ teaspoon cream of tartar
Dash salt
4 cups (1 pound) powdered sugar, sifted
1 tablespoon gum arabic, optional

In a mixing bowl, combine egg whites, cream of tartar, and salt; beat until stiff peaks form. Stir together powdered sugar and gum arabic, if desired. Gradually add powdered sugar mixture to meringue mixture, beating until stiff peaks form.

*Available at cake decorating supply outlets.

Decorating Techniques

The three most important things to remember when decorating cakes are consistency of the icing, hand position, and pressure applied to the decorating bag.

Generally speaking, use a stiff icing for flowers, a medium icing for borders and leaves, and a thinner icing for a smooth flow when writing or making stems.

The most often used hand positions for holding the decorating bag are the 45° and 90° angles. Hold the bag perpendicular to the decorating surface gripping the bag with your right hand and guiding it with the fingers of your left hand.

In the 45° angle the decorating bag is held midway between the perpendicular and the decorating surface.

When making decorations, desired effects are achieved according to the amount of pressure applied to the decorating bag. Pressure is sometimes varied during the application of a decoration, perhaps beginning with even, heavy pressure and ending with a light pressure or a release and a quick jerk up to break off icing. Pressure control and steadiness in guiding the decorating bag are the two most important things to practice to achieve the best decorating results.

Following are instructions for making various decorations found in this book.

Stems Stems are made with round opening tips. To make stems, hold the bag at a 45° angle and touch the tip directly to the surface of the icing. Apply pressure while bringing the bag up about 2 inches from the surface. As a steady stream of icing flows from the tip, move the bag in a curved direction towards the base of the stem. When using smaller opening tips, thin the icing slightly for even flow.

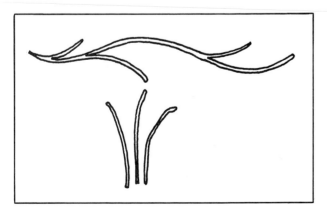

Writing Writing, either cursive or block, is done with round opening tips. Tips 1 and 2 are used most often. Thin the icing slightly when using these smaller opening tips. For professional-looking cursive writing, make the letters elongated and fairly close together.

Happy Birthday

HAPPY BIRTHDAY

Leaves Leaves are made with any of the leaf opening tips, such as 349, 350, and 352. To make leaves, hold the bag at a 45° angle and apply heavy pressure while moving the tip away. Decrease pressure as you move, bringing the leaf to a point and pulling quickly away to break off. To make a ridged leaf, simply move the bag up and down slightly while forming the leaf.

To make long leaves, such as cattail or jonquil leaves, touch the tip to the surface of the icing and apply heavy pressure. Decrease pressure slightly as you move the tip the desired length of the leaf. Release pressure and pull away quickly to make the point.

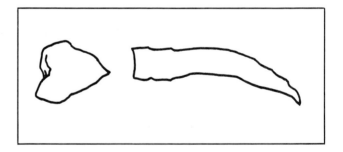

How to Make Flowers

Following are instructions for flowers used in this book.

For last-minute use, flowers can be made with Flower Decorator Icing and placed in the freezer until set before transferring directly to cake.

Flowers made of Royal Icing can be placed on the cake 1 hour after being made by placing the flowers on a metal tray and drying in the oven at 100° F. for 15 to 60 minutes or until dry enough to handle. Do not use this method for flowers made of Flower Decorator Icing which contains shortening and will melt in the oven.

Star Flowers

Make ahead using Royal Icing or directly on the cake using Buttercream Icing. These flowers make excellent fill-ins. Use tip 16, 22, or 32.

1. Attach a star tip and fill decorating bag half full with icing.
2. Hold the bag at a 90° angle (perpendicular) to the decorating surface with the tip directly on the surface.
3. Apply moderate pressure, holding the bag perfectly still.
4. Release pressure and pull tip away.
5. Follow step 5 under Drop Flowers.

Drop Flowers

These flowers can be made ahead using Royal Icing or directly on the cake using Buttercream Icing. The technique is the same using either of the icings. Use tip 224, 225, or 190.

1. Attach drop flower tip and fill decorating bag half full with icing.
2. Hold the bag at a 90° angle (perpendicular) to the decorating surface with the tip directly on the surface.
3. Apply moderate pressure, turning the bag a quarter turn as the icing emerges.
4. Release pressure and raise the tip straight up and break off icing with a quick jerk.
5. To finish, use a small round opening tip to pipe several dots of icing in a contrasting color into center of flowers, or use tip 233 to fill the centers with one motion.

Jonquils

Make Jonquils with Flower Decorator or Royal Icing. Prepare two bags of yellow icing, one with a #352 tip and the other with a #4 tip. Fill a parchment bag with yellow icing and cut a small opening in the end.

1. Secure a small square of waxed paper to a #7 flower nail.
2. Hold the bag with the #352 tip at a 45° angle, make two petals opposite each other.
3. Fill in four more petals, two on each side of the first two petals.
4. With the #4 tip, form a spiral in the center of the petals, widening the diameter slightly as you near the top of the spiral.
5. Use the parchment bag to trim the top edge of the spiral by gently wiggling the bag as the icing emerges.
6. Dry flowers completely before arranging on cake.

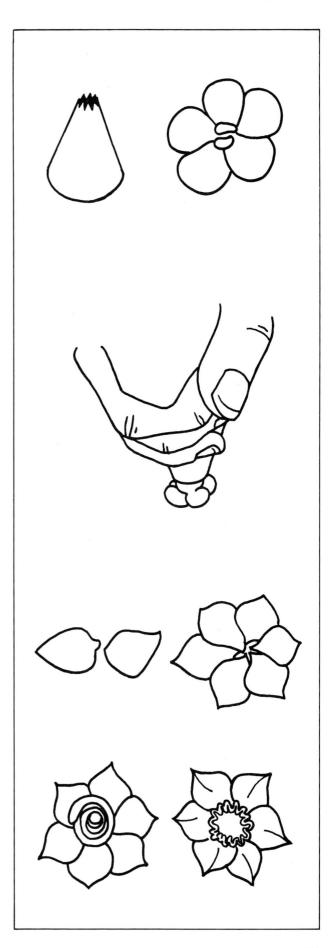

Violets

Make violets using Royal Icing. Prepare a decorating bag with tip 101 and purple icing. Fit another bag with tip 1 and yellow icing.

1. Secure a small square of waxed paper to a #2 flower nail with a dot of icing.
2. Hold the bag with tip 101 at a 45° angle with the wide end of the tip touching the nail.
3. Apply pressure, moving the tip up slightly and pivoting the tip down to the base.
4. Repeat for 4 more petals, beginning each just under the edge of the preceding petal.
5. Remove from flower nail. Pipe tip 1 dot center. Dry completely before using.

Poinsettias

Poinsettias can be made with Flower Decorator or Royal Icing. Prepare one decorating bag with a #352 tip and red icing. Make three parchment bags; fill one with green icing, one with red icing, and the third with yellow icing. Cut small opening in each bag.

1. Secure a small square of waxed paper to a #7 flower nail.
2. Starting about ½ inch from the center of the nail, form elongated leaves in a circle.
3. Moving closer to the center of the nail, add a second row of leaves, making them shorter than the first row.
4. Pipe a cluster of small green balls in the center of the red leaves, using green icing.
5. Add tiny yellow balls on the tops of each green ball, using the bag with yellow icing.
6. Top each yellow ball with a dot of red icing.
7. Dry flowers completely before arranging on top of cake.

Daisies

Daisies are easiest to form if made with Royal Icing. Prepare a decorating bag with tip 104 and white icing. Fit another bag with tip 4 and yellow icing.

1. Secure a small square of waxed paper to a #7 flower nail with a dot of icing.
2. Make a small dot of icing in the center of the waxed paper.
3. Position tip almost parallel to the surface of the nail with the narrow end toward the center of the nail.
4. Apply heavy pressure and bring the petal from the outside edge toward the center dot, gradually releasing pressure as petals form.
5. Make at least 12 petals. Remove daisy from nail.
6. Use the #4 tip and yellow icing to make yellow centers.

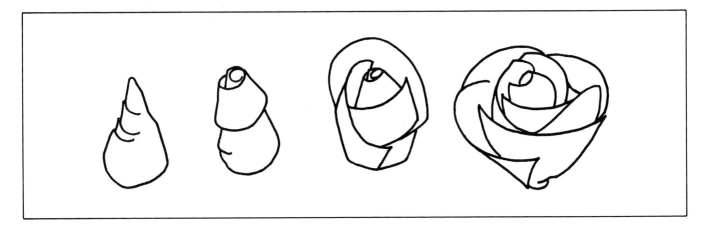

Roses

Roses can be made with Flower Decorator, Buttercream, or Royal Icing. Prepare a decorating bag with tip 104 and your choice of icing. Secure a small square of waxed paper to a #7 flower nail.

1. Make a foundation by holding the wide end of the tip at a 30° angle to the nail with the wide end touching the nail. Without moving the tip, turn the nail counterclockwise while applying pressure to form a cone. If cone is not solid, apply another layer of icing.

OR

Using the coupler only without a tip, pipe a cone of icing onto the center of the nail, holding the bag perpendicular to the nail, applying pressure and then decreasing as icing emerges.

2. Holding the nail in the left hand, lightly place the wide end of the tip just below the top center of the cone of icing.
3. While rolling the nail counterclockwise, apply pressure and form the center, tipping the tip slightly inward so that the second cone will have a small center hole at the top. Without stopping, bring the band of icing to the base of the first cone.
4. With the wide end of the tip down and keeping the tip parallel to the cone, add three overlapping petals, each of which should cover about one half of the center of the rose. To do this, press the wide end of the tip lightly against the icing at the base of the cone, close to the nail. Apply pressure and, turning the nail counterclockwise, form the three overlapping petals, arching the band of icing to make the petals almost as tall as the center.
5. Make four more overlapping petals. Start at the base, tipping the narrow end of the tip out slightly to form a more open petal that will roll at the top. Turn the nail to lengthen the petals and move the tip up slightly for height.

6. Slip the waxed paper with the completed rose onto a tray to dry.

Rosebuds

Make with Buttercream or Royal Icing. Prepare a decorating bag with tip 104 and desired color icing.

1. Hold the wide end of tip down and at a 45° angle. Apply pressure, and while moving the tip ¼ inch to the right, lift slightly and continue to apply light pressure, while moving left ¼ inch. Release pressure and pull away sharply to break off.
2. Make an overlapping petal by inserting the tip into the center of the first petal, the narrow end of the tip pointing upward.
3. Apply pressure to attach to first petal and continue pressure as the petal forms over the first petal.
4. Touch the first petal with the newly made petal and wiggle the tip slightly to detach.

Pansies

Make pansies with Flower Decorator or Royal Icing. Prepare a decorating bag with icing in desired color and tip 104.

1. Secure a small square of waxed paper to a #7 flower nail with a dot of icing.
2. Position the tip at a 45° angle with the wide end touching the center of the nail and the narrow end raised slightly and pointed to the left.
3. Apply pressure and swivel bag to the right, keeping the wide end down and the narrow end raised slightly.
4. Release with a sharp, upward pull.
5. Make another lay down petal, partially overlapping the first petal.
6. Make 2 more petals directly on top of the first two petals, side by side.
7. Make a large ruffled petal by placing the wide end of the tip at the base of the formed petals and applying heavy pressure while turning the nail, without turning the tip.
8. Remove flower from nail. Dry completely on waxed paper. Use an artist brush and purple food color to add veins.

Easter Lilies

Easter Lilies should be made with Royal Icing. Prepare a decorating bag with tip 352 and white icing.

1. Cut a 3-inch square piece of aluminum foil. Fit the foil into a #12 flower nail. Grease heavily with shortening.
2. Place tip in the center of the nail. Apply pressure, pulling the tip out of the center and bringing it up slightly over the rim.
3. Release pressure and pull away quickly to form a point.
4. Make a petal directly opposite the first petal.
5. Fill in with two more petals on each side of the first petals. Leave center somewhat open.
6. Insert artificial stamens in the center or pipe tip 1 yellow dots.
7. Carefully remove foil from the nail. Dry completely before removing foil.

Decorative Borders

For most borders, Buttercream Frosting works very well. For special cakes, such as wedding or anniversary cakes, Boiled Icing is very good since it makes sharp, white decorations. Boiled Icing is excellent for string work. Except for string work, do not use Royal Icing for borders, since it becomes very hard.

Dot Border

Dot borders can be made with any round opening tip. Tip 6 works well for an average size cake.

How to Make a Dot Border

1. Fit any round opening tip (2 through 12) into a pastry bag. Fill halfway with icing.
2. Hold bag perpendicular to the surface and about ⅛ inch above.
3. Apply pressure so that icing flows around the tip, but do not move tip.
4. Release pressure and pull tip away. Continue making dots around top or bottom edge of cake.

Shell Border

One of the most commonly used borders, it can be made with Buttercream or Boiled Icing.

How to Make Shell Borders

1. Fit any star tip (such as 16, 22, or 32) into a pastry bag. Fill halfway with icing.
2. Hold the bag perpendicular to and about ⅙ inch above the surface.
3. Apply pressure, moving the tip foward about ⅛ inch, increasing pressure as you move the tip. Pull the tip down and out as pressure is released.
4. Begin the next shell near the end of the last one, pushing back gently into the shell as it builds up until it barely covers the tail of the last shell.

Star Border

A very simple border easily made with any star tip.

How to a Make a Star Border

1. Fit any star tip (such as 16, 22, or 32) into a pastry bag. Fill halfway with icing.
2. Hold the bag perpendicular to the surface and barely touching the surface.
3. Apply enough pressure to secure the star to the surface. Too much pressure will result in loss of shape.
4. Release pressure and remove tip.
5. Continue making stars around top or bottom edge of cake.

String Border

Make with any round opening tip. Tip 2 is the most commonly used.

How to Make a String Border

1. Fit a decorating bag with any round opening tip. Fill halfway with icing.
2. Hold the bag perpendicular to the surface.
3. Touch the surface lightly to attach the string. Continue pressure, pulling the tip to the desired length and swinging it to the right

before touching the side of the cake. It is important to remember that the string should hang naturally. Do not attempt to draw it directly on the cake.

Bulb and Drop Border

This is a simple combination of two other border techniques, the dot border and the string border.

How to Make a Bulb and Drop Border

1. Fit a decorating bag with tip 4. Fill halfway with Boiled or Buttercream Icing.
2. Pipe a dot at the top of the cake side, keeping the tube under the surface of the icing. Without releasing pressure, pull a string straight out about 1¼ to 1½ inches from the dot.
3. Bring the string across and attach it to the top of the cake as desired.

4. Midway between the ball and the end of the string, make another dot. Pull out a string the same length as the first and attach it just beyond the next dot.
5. Tuck the end of the last string under the first string to finish the border.

Heart Border

This border is made with any round opening tip. Tip 6 works well on an average size cake.

How to Make a Heart Border

1. Fit a decorating bag with any round opening tip. Fill halfway with icing.
2. Hold the bag perpendicular to and about ¹⁄₁₆ inch away from surface.
3. Apply pressure, moving the tip up and to the left and increasing pressure at the uppermost point.

4. Decrease pressure and move tip down to form a tear drop, touching the surface at the lower end.
5. Repeat procedure as above working from the right and downward.

Reverse Scroll Border

Use tip 16 for a small border; tip 32 for a large border.

How to Make Reverse Scroll Borders

1. Fit a pastry bag with a star tip. Fill halfway with icing.
2. Hold the bag at a 45° angle to the surface.
3. Apply steady pressure to make a sideways number 6.

4. Without releasing pressure, reverse to make a sideways number 9.
5. Continue making border, alternating figures, and without releasing pressure.

Frame Border

1. Fit a decorating bag with tip 104. Fill halfway with icing.
2. Hold the tip nearly flat against the cake with the wide end ¼ inch from the outside edge of the cake and the narrow end toward the outside edge and slightly raised.
3. Apply even pressure, make an arch, three short jiggles of the tip, another curve, and three more jiggles.
4. Repeat until the cake is completely framed.

Swag Border

For the most uniform swags, use a commercial swag marker available at cake decorating outlets or mark the side of the cake lightly with a toothpick before making the border. To divide the sides of the cake into even sections, cut a piece of waxed paper the same size as the cake top and fold in eighths. Place the paper on the cake top and make a light mark at each fold.

How to Make a Wiggle Swag Border

1. Fit a decorating bag with tip 16 or tip 88. Fill halfway with icing.
2. Hold the bag at the side of the cake at a 45° angle. If using tip 88, the star end of the tip should be touching the cake and the flat end away from the cake.
3. Apply pressure, wiggling the tip up and down as you form the swag.

How to Make a Smooth Swag Border

1. Fit a decorating bag with tip 103 or 104. Fill halfway with icing.
2. Hold the bag at the side of the cake with the wide end touching the cake.
3. Apply pressure and arch the swag down to the right and then up in a quick, smooth motion until it reaches the end of the section.

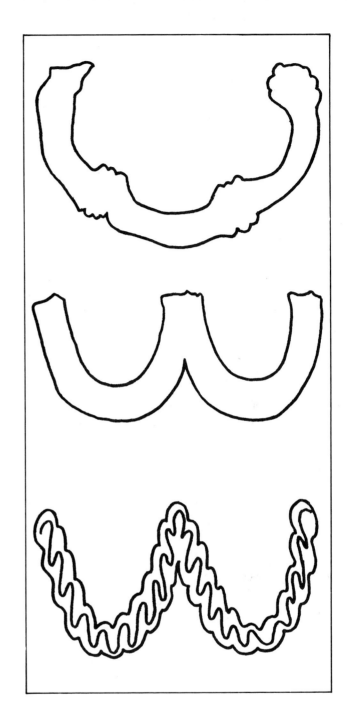

Piping Gel

Piping gel is available clear and in colors. It is more practical to purchase clear gel and add the desired paste color as needed. Piping gel is too soft for flowers or borders, but it is excellent for writing, water in scene painting (such as lakes, below), and church windows. Following are some ideas used in this book that most effectively use piping gel.

Dots Fill a pastry bag fitted with tip 2 and pipe dots as desired between shells or scallops in a border.

Lakes After icing the cake, let stand until icing has formed a crust. Spread blue piping gel in the desired area to form a lake.

Pictures To make pictures, piping gel is used on rice paper, a paper-like edible product, onto which a pattern is traced and then placed on the cake. It is available at cake decorating supply outlets. Follow the instructions below to make piping gel pictures.

1. Place the rice paper over the desired picture, taping the rice paper lightly to keep it from moving.
2. Trace the picture onto the rice paper with a non-toxic pencil or pen.
3. Remove the rice paper from the original picture.
4. Cover the rice paper using a ½-inch artist brush and clear piping gel.
5. Using a small brush, dip it into the desired paste color and blend into the areas to be painted on the rice paper. Use only a small amount of paste color to avoid harsh and overly vivid colors. If the area to be colored has begun to dry, apply a little more clear piping gel before painting.
6. Let rice paper picture stand overnight to dry. Trim with manicuring scissors.
7. Place picture on cake.

Stencils

Stencils are an easy, neat way to design a cake top. Any pattern can be used, following these basic steps.

1. Trace the desired pattern onto a piece of stiff paper, such as poster paper.
2. Carefully cut out pattern.
3. Ice the cake and let stand until a crust forms.
4. Place the stencil on top of the cake.
5. Using the same icing as the cake was frosted in, soften the icing with a few drops of water. Spread the thinned icing over the stencil.
6. Carefully lift the stencil straight up from the cake.
7. Decorate the stencil design as desired.

Figure Piping

Figure piping is a simple but creative way to cleverly design cakes. To figure pipe, use Buttercream, Royal, or Boiled Icing in a parchment bag or a pastry bag fitted with any round opening tip 1 through 12. For upright or bulky figures, use Boiled or Royal Icing to pipe figures directly on the cake. To make figures in advance, use Royal Icing and pipe figures onto waxed paper.

Because of the length of time required to mix and fill several different bags, it is a good idea to make the figure piped characters in advance using all of the icing and simply store any remaining figures for later use.

For detailed instructions on how to figure pipe the delightful characters in this book, see individual instructions.

Candy Molding

Candy molds are usually made of durable clear plastic and are available in a wide choice of designs. Candy molds can be purchased at cake and candy supply outlets. The molds are filled with melted candy coating to create delightful designs that will enhance any cake design.

How to Candy Mold

1. Fill bottom of a double boiler with water and bring to a boil. Remove from heat.
2. Place top of double boiler over water. Place candy coating in double boiler. (If using block coating, chop into small pieces.) Let stand, stirring occasionally, until coating is melted and smooth. *Alternate Method:* To melt in a microwave oven, place coating in a microsafe bowl in the microwave. Microwave on high for 1 minute. Stir; microwave 1 minute. Stir until smooth.
3. Spoon or pour melted coating into a clean dry mold.
4. Place mold in freezer until mold feels cold and appears slightly cloudy.
5. Remove from freezer and turn molded piece out of mold. *Note:* If molded piece does not turn out immediately, return to freezer and repeat above procedure.

Painted Molds

Molds containing more details can be "painted" with melted candy coating. Place the colored candy wafers in small glass or metal containers and place in a larger container filled with hot water. Baby food jars are ideal, since they can simply be covered and stored if there is any remaining coating. Another method is to use a muffin pan, placing a different color in each compartment. Place the muffin pan in a large pan filled with hot water on the stove over very low heat. Do not allow water or steam to mix with coating.

To paint the mold, use a fine artist brush such as #0 to #0000. If painting two different colors adjacent to each other, first paint one color and then place the mold in the freezer to set the coating before painting the next color.

After painting the mold as desired, fill with any solid color melted coating. Or, paint with a thin coat of the solid color and chill. Fill with any filling such as maple or caramel. Seal with melted coating. Chill for a few minutes before turning out of mold.

Three-Dimensional Hollow Molds

These molds are made with two parts. First paint the features on each half of the mold as above. Then fill one half of the mold with chocolate and clip the mold together. Turn the mold to distribute the chocolate evenly over the inside of the mold. Stand in freezer until set, about 3 minutes. Turn the mold again to distribute chocolate and return to freezer for 3 minutes. Repeat once again, returning to the freezer until completely set, about 15 minutes for an average size mold.

Molds should always be stood upright in freezer so that excess chocolate will flow to the bottom of the mold.

Remove mold from chocolate pieces and trim seam if necessary. Handle as little as possible to avoid fingerprints.

Solid Three-Dimensional Molds

Paint inside as above. Fill one half of the mold completely with coating. Place in freezer until set. Remove from freezer. Fill remaining half of mold with melted coating. Place chilled half on top. Clip together securely. Place in freezer until set. Remove mold and trim seam if necessary.

Run Sugar

Patterns can be chosen from art or coloring books as long as the lines are distinct enough to be clearly seen through waxed paper.

1. Place the pattern on a flat, sturdy surface which can be moved later. Do not tape the pattern down.
2. Cover the pattern with waxed paper and secure the waxed paper with tape. Select colors to be used and color small amount of Royal Icing. Thin remaining icing with a few drops of water so that when dropped from a spoon onto waxed paper a soft peak smooths itself in 3 to 4 seconds. Fill parchment bags with icings. Cut small holes in tips of bags. Fold tops down securely.
3. Color a small portion of Royal Icing black and fill a pastry bag fitted with tip 2.
4. Outline picture with black icing.
5. Flood outlined areas, working quickly from side to side, so that no area dries so much that it will not flow together. Be sure that the run sugar comes up to the outline, barely covers it, but does not flow beyond it. Mound icing slightly in the center of the area being filled. Watch for low areas and fill in. Unevenness will cause weak spots in the finished piece.
6. Let stand until completely dry, usually about 24 hours.
7. Cut the tape on one side of the waxed paper and slide the pattern from under the run sugar piece.
8. Paint details with a fine brush and food coloring. Dry completely.
9. To remove from waxed paper, move the piece to the edge of the table, pulling gently on the waxed paper. Hold one hand under the piece and with the other hand, pull the waxed paper from the bottom, working from side to side.

Pattern can be made with run sugar directly on the cake for last-minute work and will dry sufficiently in about 1 hour to be lightly painted with food coloring. Center will be soft.

Royal Icing Heads

Run sugar heads made with thinned Royal Icing can be used with figure piped characters. See page 27 for detailed instructions.

Index

Index of Cakes
(By category and in order of appearance)

Index of Decorating Techniques